Speaking

with

BOLD ASSURANCE

How to Become a Persuasive Communicator

Bert Decker
&
Hershael W. York

BROADMAN
& HOLMAN
PUBLISHERS

Nashville, Tennessee

0-8054-2210-2

Published by Broadman & Holman Publishers, Nashville, Tennessee

Dewey Decimal Classification: 261.5
Subject Heading: ORAL COMMUNICATION—RELIGIOUS
ASPECTS—CHRISTIANITY
Library of Congress Card Catalog Number: 00-060814

Unless otherwise stated all Scripture citation is from the NIV, the Holy Bible, New International Version, copyright © 1973, 1978, 1984 by International Bible Society. Other versions cited are NASB, the New American Standard Bible, © the Lockman Foundation, 1960, 1962, 1963, 1968, 1971, 1972, 1973, 1975, 1977; used by permission; and the King James Version.

The Decker Grid System™ is a registered trademark.

Library of Congress Cataloging-in-Publication Data
Decker, Bert.
   Speaking with bold assurance : how to become a persuasive communicator / Bert Decker and Hershael W. York.
      p. cm.
   ISBN 0-8054-2210-2 (pb)
      1. Oral communication—Religious aspects—Christianity. I. York,
   Hershael W., 1960– II. Title.
BV4597.53.C64 D43   2001
261.5—dc21

                                                         00-060814
                                                         CIP

1 2 3 4 5 6 7 8 9 10   05 04 03 02 01

For a special family: My wife, Dru Scott, whom I love very much, and who is also my favorite author and speaker. Our faithful children, Allison, Sam, Harold, Shannon, and Kelly. And all of their dear children, the growing joys of our lives—Ashley, Taja, Aaron, Haley, Brandon, Mariah, and Kyle.

—Bert Decker

For Tanya, the greatest communicator I know, because she daily conveys the thousands of ways she loves me.

—Herschael York

Contents

Part I
Why Bold Assurance?

Bold Assurance is an exciting new concept that builds speaking skills and confidence with God-given principles. Although *Speaking with Bold Assurance* will be useful for anyone, it is specifically geared for Christians who want to share God's Word and precepts effectively, whether in the boardroom, the classroom, at church, or at home.

> *For God did not give us a spirit of timidity, but a spirit of power, of love and of self-discipline.*
> 2 TIMOTHY 1:7

First, bold assurance is for the lay Christian. People in all walks of life are afraid of speaking before groups or under pressure. Christians often appear to be even more timid in their speaking, particularly about their faith—faith which should be the bedrock of their being.

> *God did not create us to put audiences to sleep, but to wake them up to the hope and glory of His way.*
> JOHN MAXWELL,
> PARAPHRASED

Second, bold assurance is for Christian leaders. Leaders in business continue to write and read speeches and dump data when they could create and inspire with thoughts and stories. And pastors and preachers, whose primary business is speaking, even more so tend to compose and read sermon manuscripts rather than inspire and motivate their listeners with the natural power of speech.

> *For the LORD will be your confidence . . .*
> PROVERBS 3:26

There have been thousands of books on speaking and hundreds on preaching, but none has combined a practical and proven methodology for speaking effectively with God's Word. The Bible tells us how God wants us to be communicators. Bold Assurance is the concept that combines these principles in ways that help you communicate more effectively. *Speaking with Bold Assurance* captures these concepts in one easy-to-read-and-implement book.

> *Now go; I will help you speak and will teach you what to say.*
> EXODUS 4:12

CHAPTER I

Introduction

God spoke. He spoke in Creation when he said, "Let there be light." He spoke through his prophets who said, "Thus says the Lord . . ." He spoke to us through his Word, the perfect revelation of who he is and his will for our lives. Most of all, he spoke through Jesus Christ, his only Son, who came to reveal God's love for an undeserving sinful world.

And God wants to speak *through you*. He has placed you in a network of family, friends, coworkers, neighbors, and acquaintances that *only you* are uniquely positioned and qualified to touch and to reach. But if you are like most people, you sometimes feel intimidated into silence.

Have you ever sensed an opportunity to share a spiritual insight with someone, but you weren't sure you could say it just right so you kept the truth to yourself? Have you ever lost a sale or a business relationship because you did not know how to express that you really *are* the best person for the job? Has God ever given you a perfect opportunity to share the gospel with someone you have been praying for, yet you remained quietly ashamed because you did not feel adequate to give him the very thing he most needed? Have you ever declined to teach a class because you were afraid to speak to a group?

This book is for everyone who hungers to be a more effective communicator of God's truth, whether you are sharing yourself, your life, your story, or your insight into the Scriptures. Whether speaking to a large group or to just one person, the powerful principles of communication that we have put into this book will make you more comfortable and competent in speaking.

We are committed to helping God's people convey God's truth in a manner consistent with the magnificent message that is ours to share. But we are also committed to helping God's people share *themselves* in a way that establishes trust and credibility for *all* situations. Though there are many secular books and programs available that can help anyone be a better communicator (some of which we have written!), there is a critical need for a book with the Christian message, ministry, and lifestyle at its core.

If you read and follow the potent principles in this book, you will learn to:

- Talk to anyone, anytime
- Share your faith with others
- Create and organize ideas
- Enhance your credibility
- Overcome stage fright
- Persuade others
- Make your point
- Think on your feet
- Avoid being intimidated
- Communicate with authority
- Give your testimony

The result of combining God's Word with proven and practical skills to increase your speaking effectiveness is *bold assurance*. As you commit yourself to communicating his truth, be prepared to experience God using you more powerfully and more frequently than ever before.

CHAPTER 2
What God Says

Most Christians would be shocked to discover how much God says in his Word about communicating. The common theme in almost all of those passages, however, is *power*—complete confidence in *God's* power.

Paul, for instance, reminded the Corinthian believers that he came to them "in weakness and fear, and with much trembling" (1 Cor. 2:3), but that was only how he *felt*, not how he came across. They witnessed that his "message and [his] preaching were not with wise and persuasive words, but with a demonstration of the Spirit's power," and they believed because their faith rested on that demonstration of God's power conveyed through Paul's demeanor (1 Cor. 2:4–5).

THE POWER IS IN THE PASSION

Many people have used this passage to teach exactly the opposite of what Paul is saying. They argue that since Paul seems to be decrying the rhetoric and technique of his contemporaries, we should not employ any type of human methodology at all. The power, they argue, rests solely in the *content* of the message, never in the *communication* of that message.

The question we must ask and answer, therefore, is what exactly *was* the demonstration of power to which Paul referred. If we really believed that *only* content mattered, then we would have no need of anything but written communication. Pastors could merely mail manuscripts of messages to their members. Sunday school teachers could simply have students read the lessons or study guide. Sales personnel would never have to meet with potential customers; they could just E-mail them the information.

No, as important as content is—and it is essential and central to communication—it needs a conduit of communication, a method of transmitting it from one person to another. No one knew that better than those who heard the apostle Paul preach.

Picture what his first-century hearers witnessed. Perhaps he was scarred, having suffered beatings, flogging, stoning, and the ravages of life on the road in an inhospitable environment. Tradition holds that he suffered near blindness. His life and freedom were threatened every time he opened his mouth to preach the gospel. His listeners might scorn him or slight him, imprison or behead him, yet he would not be intimidated into silence nor retreat. No personal discomfort would diminish his passion. He was not afraid of any consequence except disobedience to the will of God.

This kind of fearlessness in the face of imminent danger has always won an audience. People are moved by men and women who feel their message is worth the risk of death. *That* is a demonstration of power!

What Is Bold Assurance?

God wants his message not only to have the right content, but to have a power that is palpable. In other words, God desires bold assurance in his message.

How do you picture bold assurance? One image is of a person speaking with confidence and certainty about something he believes deeply and passionately. He is authentic, and he is effective.

Why can't we all speak with bold assurance? We all have things we are passionate about—concepts, ideals, faith, business opportunities, presentations—and yet we so often undermine ourselves in the way we speak about these concerns. Not confident, not certain, and certainly not effective. Why is that?

What keeps us from being all that we can be in this most critical area—communicating with effectiveness to the people in our lives?

The answer is simple—fear. Public speaking is listed as the number-one fear in this country, but for the believer it does not have to be that way.

The Disciples' Fear

The most fearful people of all were eleven men and a handful of women two thousand years ago when Jesus Christ was crucified on the cross. This should have been a bold group. They had actually seen the miracles done; they had experienced their leader firsthand. Peter denied Jesus Christ three times out of his own fear of persecution. And this small band of followers was so fearful and terrified that they hid after the Crucifixion.

They had not always been so fearful. In fact, just days before the Crucifixion they were filled with the Spirit of God and filled with faith, as the Bible tells us in Luke 19:

> When he came near the place where the road goes down to the Mount of Olives, the whole crowd of disciples began joyfully to praise God in loud voices for all the miracles they had seen: "Blessed is the king who comes in the name of the Lord!" "Peace in heaven and glory in the highest!" Some of the Pharisees in the crowd said to Jesus, "Teacher, rebuke your disciples." "I tell you," he replied, "if they keep quiet, the stones will cry out." (vv. 37–40)

The disciples were shouting for joy, praising the Lord, believing, fully confident in the miracles that Jesus had done and in him as the Son of God.

A few days later they scattered, fearful. And it wasn't just Peter and the disciples who were confused, afraid, and losing faith at this time; it was also the women who had played a very important role. Mark 16:8 reads, "Trembling and bewildered, the women went out and fled from the tomb. They said nothing to anyone, because they were afraid."

Why did God allow them to lack the confidence they should have had by this time? There's a reason for this, even though it seems to go against how we might think or want God to act.

WE HAVE A CHOICE

We have a choice—to choose fear or to choose confidence. Which gives every one of us—no matter what our present level of personal confidence—great hope. For we *can* choose to be confident.

Why then are we so nervous, fearful, or afraid? Why are we too often thinking that we are inadequate? Why is there such difficulty with people being struck with terror or fear when they have to get up in front of others to speak about what they could easily say to one person? Why do we make so many excuses that allow this fear to either hinder us or in some cases overwhelm us?

There are several reasons for this. First, fear comes from the psychological fight-or-flight response that occurs in the human being whenever confronted by danger. The fight-or-flight response is real because we want to be able to react quickly to actual danger and either take flight—flee from it—or fight it. This is natural, and God gave us this response as a useful tool. But too often we let terror or fear overwhelm us, when it is really adrenaline that could enable us to physically act and perform more effectively.

Fear is just misapplied adrenaline. It is like the athlete before the championship match. He or she has "fear," adrenaline, which gives power and life to the performance. If there is no adrenaline, there is a lesser, flat performance, so there is a good purpose in applying that fight-or-flight response appropriately. The fear response can be a good thing.

But we have altered it when it comes to speaking. Too often we make speaking before others seem a threat—a danger. Even though others can't really harm us, we think they can because they are going to be judging us—so we want to either flee or fight. Neither response is appropriate. We have to talk!

SHYNESS

Shyness is a sin.

Now that the weight of that statement has settled a bit, it begs some qualification and explanation. First, we aren't talking about pathological shyness, which affects a very small percentage of people (about 4 percent) who suffer from a timidity rooted in neurological or traumatic causes. When we say that it is a sin to be shy, what we mean is that those who use shyness as a crutch, an excuse to keep silent with their message, are disobedient to God and more concerned with their personal comfort or image. It is best put in 2 Timothy 1:7, "For God did not give us a spirit of timidity, but a spirit of power, of love and of self-discipline." And Jesus himself warned us about hiding our light under a bushel!

God never has accepted excuses for failing to share his Word. Moses tried hiding behind a speech impediment. God responded by reminding his servant Moses that he was the one who made man's mouth. No one knows our weaknesses and perceived limitations better than our Maker. He knows all of the difficulties that we run to hide behind. He chose our families, the places of our birth, our environments and influences, and our precise genetic makeup. Even the tragedies and difficulties of our lives have been filtered through his love and are a part of his providential care for us.

In our society and in our backgrounds, we have a cultural grace toward those who are humble and shy. But it's important to see God's perspective from his Word, and to see this right at the outset, because it's not necessarily aligned with our culture and natural inclinations.

Shyness is also very ineffective. Some degree of shyness is common to most of us; we are all threatened and intimidated somewhat when we are in new relationships—meeting new people—in unfamiliar situations. What we want to do is withdraw and get with the familiar. We want to shrink in, rather than expand out.

When his area manager retired, Benton was one of a small number who had the experience and ability to step in and take the company to greater productivity and sales. And as a Christian, he also knew he could exert a positive moral influence on the entire organization. By making some key decisions and living out his own values in the workplace, he had the opportunity to directly influence employees and their families. He would even have a greater platform from which to share the gospel as occasion afforded itself.

But first he had to present himself to the board and convince the board members that he alone was the best choice for the job. The thought of so much riding on a one-hour presentation in front of twenty-four men and women who would be judging everything he said and did panicked him. Oppressed by his own fear, Benton decided to endure the lifelong disappointment of what could have been rather than choosing to face his own fear and turn it into positive energy and passion.

So God allows us to do battle, but he wants us to make the right choice, the choice that will give us victory. Remember the disciples who fled in fear and confusion after the Crucifixion? Their choice wasn't one of victory then, for they were not filled with the Spirit. But Peter and John changed and made a different choice a short time later, when they began speaking about what they believed. The rulers and elders didn't know what to do with them and even threw them in prison because they were gaining too many followers.

In Acts 4 Peter and John reacted as the rulers and elders said, "'. . . to stop this thing from spreading any further among the people, we must warn these men to speak no longer to anyone in this name.' Then they called them in again and commanded them not to speak or teach at all in the name of Jesus. But Peter and John replied, 'Judge for yourselves whether it is right in God's sight to obey you rather than God. For we cannot help speaking about what we have seen and heard'" (vv. 17–20).

God gives us that choice between being filled with fear or confidence, timidity or boldness, so we can make the choice ourselves—and see that we must rely on him when we do choose confidence and boldness.

In truth, the comfort that comes from disobedience is only temporary. After the initial relief of refusing to reach out comes the guilt that silent Christianity breeds. Permanent peace and victory over fear can come only when we rise above them by choosing God's way.

There Is Hope

Here is where the hope comes in. We can have bold assurance and be excited about the confidence and the certainty that God gives us. One of the keys to unlocking this is in Psalm 147:10–11: "His pleasure is not in the strength of the horse, nor his delight in the legs of a man; the LORD delights in those who fear him, who put their hope in his unfailing love."

This is echoed throughout the Bible whenever the Lord wanted people to put their trust in him. He wants us to be able to rely on him. There can be nothing clearer throughout both the Old and New Testaments. God wants us to be humble in ourselves but confident and certain in him. And with that certainty we can then have bold assurance.

Sheila was shocked when she discovered that her ten-year-old son could check out pornographic materials at the local library. In her heart she knew that she had to do something to change that policy, but if it meant speaking to the city council, she wasn't sure she could do it. She wasn't accustomed to speaking to groups in a public forum.

But as she prayed about it, Sheila became convinced that no one could have as much impact on the council as a concerned mother. Relying on the Lord's promise to be with her, she wrote all of the council members a kind but straightforward letter and then appeared at the next city council meeting. By choosing to speak up rather than to be intimidated into silence, her impassioned and well-reasoned plea for common sense so moved the council that it instructed the library to change its policy so that parents had to approve of any sensitive material before a child could check it out. By relying on God's strength and choosing to defeat her shyness, Sheila had impacted her entire community.

CHAPTER 3

How to Reach the World

When God wanted us to know of his great love for us, how did he get the most important message in the world to us? The author of the book of Hebrews wrote, "In the past God spoke to our forefathers through the prophets at many times and in various ways, but in these last days he has spoken to us by his Son, . . ." (Heb. 1:1–2). In other words, the most effective personal communication is precisely that—the communication of a *person*.

COMMUNICATING THROUGH A PERSON

God did not just write a letter—he sent his Son, Jesus Christ. Jesus did not come merely to convey a message, but to actually *be* God's message. That personal communication remains central to Christianity. In fact, as important as communication is for any human business, it is nowhere as important as in the Christian life.

When we communicate with God, we call that *prayer*. When we communicate with other Christians, we call that *fellowship*. When we communicate with unbelievers, we call that *witness*. That ability and confidence to communicate lies at the heart of Christian effectiveness. You can't be a lone Christian any more than you can have a one-man football game!

And all three—prayer, fellowship, and witness—use words to communicate. The base is the written word of the Bible, but most often when that Word makes the difference in communicating with others, and particularly in witnessing, it is spoken. Remember Romans 10:17: "Faith comes from hearing the message, and the message is heard through the word of Christ."

The great missionary and apostle Paul was a communicator extraordinaire. He exhibited such a conviction that many Gentiles who had never heard of the one true God were touched by his passion and fire. Paul's journeys left a trail of converts and churches behind—not so much because the

Gentiles were intellectually stimulated, but because they were touched by the Spirit of God through Paul.

Andrew, though not one of the best known of the twelve apostles, still filled an important function because he was the one who brought his brother, Simon Peter, to Jesus. After he came to accept Jesus as his Messiah, he immediately went and found Simon. He did not present a reasoned and logical display for his brother but passionately and convincingly announced, "We have found the Messiah!" (John 1:41).

But sharing Jesus and biblical truth is not just for supersaints and apostles. It is for you and me. Peter wrote that we should "always be prepared to give an answer to everyone who asks you to give the reason for the hope that you have" (1 Pet. 3:15). And the only way we can do that is through personal communication.

Though the gospel itself is the most important Christian message, it is by no means the only one. The Bible is filled with practical teaching and insightful wisdom that is to be shared. It informs our businesses, our boardrooms, our homes, our families, and our most intimate moments.

Your Personal Experience

Take a moment and think of the Christians who have most influenced you. Perhaps they are well-known authors or preachers, or perhaps they are family members, Sunday school teachers, or godly neighbors. Whoever they may be, there was something in them that made you believe in them and accept what they believed and modeled.

This is what ordinary Christians have in common with great preachers like Billy Graham and biblical models like the apostle Paul. It is not that we must be eloquent or educated, but that we must be passionate, confident, believable, and, therefore, persuasive.

Isn't that your personal experience? How many women accepted their future husband's proposal of marriage based on its eloquence? If that were the case, there would be far more single men! No, her acceptance is based on his conviction, not just the words that he says.

To return to the Christians who have influenced you the most, they were not necessarily the smartest Christians you ever met. They were not necessarily the most eloquent believers you ever met. But they were *real*, they were *committed*, and thus they were *powerful*.

God Wants the World Reached

Just as others have touched you, God wants you to reach, to touch, and to influence those around you. The most effective way to do that is to communicate who you *are*—and that means sharing the most dearly held beliefs that you have.

Perhaps the best-loved verse of the New Testament is John 3:16: "For God so loved the world that he gave his one and only Son, that whoever believes in him shall not perish but have eternal life."

In other words, God *communicated*—he shared his love by giving himself in the person of Jesus Christ, and now believers live in the overflow of that gift. Just as God gave himself, so we give of ourselves to those around us. And the way to do that is through effective communication.

CHAPTER 4
Personal Success

When it comes to communicating, we can choose fear or confidence when under pressure. You have heard of performance anxiety—that is something akin to this fear of speaking. Every individual has performance anxiety. What we all really want to do is to perform at our peak level when the pressure is on, and *not* have the anxiety. But that is when it is toughest. And it becomes so much easier when we rely on God and not on ourselves.

Athletes sometimes reach a level of performance that is almost unconscious. They just can't miss. You know when athletes are in a "zone"—when Michael Jordan would score fifty or sixty points in a game and couldn't miss, or when Tiger Woods won the Masters by a record twelve strokes in a most dramatic and unique performance. There are many examples of the zone in athletics.

When the pressure is on and the leverage is the highest, we want to do our best, and it is then, ironically, that our emotions flood our minds and we are not able to think clearly or behave with the confidence that we would otherwise have. But rather than thinking of that pressure as an obstacle, we need to see that it is actually the work of God. He allows the push-pull of that pressure/performance dichotomy to let us know that all we have to do is call upon him to get them in the right balance, but he wants us to call upon him.

And those who have bold assurance because of how they call out to God in dependence on him, because of who they are in Christ, filled with his spirit of power, love, and self-discipline, have the potential for a lot more zones than those who don't.

Bert:
At one of my biggest moments in giving a speech, I was at the Million Dollar Round Table. This is a large annual convention, where the top 2 percent of all the

life insurance salespeople in the world gather to learn and be motivated. It is one of the most prestigious events to which a professional speaker could be invited— I was honored, and pumped up. I will never forget sitting backstage, hearing the speaker on stage before me, looking at his projected image on the screen—about 30 feet high—hearing the laughter and roars of the audience of six thousand people, and realizing I was going on next. That is a case for high-level tension. And I had it. The adrenaline was flowing.

But I was excited and enthused to be there, and I will never forget that I had a sense of calm because I had prayed earlier that morning. When I was in my hotel room knowing what was coming up, I had a lot of tension, but it was truly stimulating because I knew that God was with me, and I prayed for power from God and turned the performance over to him.

I remember many times before when I did not know this secret of relying on God and his commands, which I was not obeying before, and how alone I felt and how difficult speeches were. That has all changed.

One of the highest tension situations I have ever faced was going on NBC's "Today" show to talk about the presidential debates. I have been privileged to be on the show many times as its communications expert, talking about who won or who lost based on their behavior. It is a great chance for exposure to talk about my communications ideas, but it's also pretty high-level tension because you only have two or three minutes to get across your ideas. You have to be spontaneous and you have to come across with high-level energy. Luckily, I train people in that so I knew what I told them to do, mechanically, but now I had to do it myself. And the mechanics are not enough to quiet the emotions.

But the interesting thing was that it was a stimulating experience, not a terrifying one. The adrenaline was flowing, but again I prayed before going on and prayed that God would be in charge. I am not saying that I thought of him all the time during the session. Actually I was thinking feverishly of what I was going to say next in response to Bryant Gumbel's or Katie Couric's questions, but I felt I was in the zone performance, with God's help.

We can always be in the zone if we rely on what God says. We can always achieve performance excellence through God's power and not through our own. In Luke 22:33 Peter told Jesus: "Lord, I am ready to go with you to prison and to death.'" Peter was ready at that time, but when the chips were down, he denied Jesus three times. He was relying on his own resources for success rather than on God's power. Later, energized by and reliant on the Holy Spirit, Peter was so bold with God's confidence that he could speak out to audiences of thousands, under all kinds of pressure, even to the point of suffering a martyr's death.

It is unlikely that you will ever be called upon to suffer physically like Peter did, but it *is* probable that God will call on you to tell your friends, your neighbors, or your coworkers what he has done for you, and for them, through Jesus Christ. You will need divine wisdom to take a stand for your convictions with your family, on the job, and in your relationships. You need the power that God gives to succeed in every endeavor of life.

LIVING RIGHT IS NOT ENOUGH

We once heard someone ask a Bible teacher about his neighbors, who were very good people but who did not believe in Jesus Christ nor in all of the principles of the Bible. They lived moral lives, however, and had good ethics. They were hard-working, and they succeeded. He asked, "Why do you need the Bible? Why do you need Jesus Christ? Why do you need faith when you can just use the principles and have a good life?"

Certainly God's principles *do* work for everyone. Anybody who uses them, whether he believes in Jesus or believes in the Bible or not, will be more successful than those who don't. God's laws are like gravity. They are written into the very fabric of the universe and are always true. God's laws in the Bible are trustworthy and available for anybody to use. There is just one difference: those who use them for temporal things will get only temporal results and will miss the blessing of seeing God's precepts at work in the eternal.

But if you add the firepower of belief and faith—the emotional commitment to their veracity, blessed by the mystery of the Holy Spirit's power—that is when you get wonders. That is when you get the super-heated success and prosperity as God defines it, and that is when you get stability and consistency as well. That is when your efforts are graced by the fruit of the Holy Spirit.

SEEK FIRST HIS KINGDOM

Another key point to realizing both kinds of success is contained in three words: Seek God first. Actually, Jesus put it more poetically and completely in his great Sermon on the Mount. In Matthew 6:33–34 he says, "'But seek first his kingdom and his righteousness, and all these things will be given to you as well. Therefore do not worry about tomorrow, for tomorrow will worry about itself. Each day has enough trouble of its own.'" In other words, as we commit ourselves to the important things, God obligates himself to take care of the necessary things and to even supply more than we need.

As we seek God's rule and reign in our lives, we are amazed to discover that we enjoy tremendous success, partly because the principles are working to cause that success, and partly because our desires themselves have been refined so that some things that once mattered no longer do. We simplify and eliminate many unnecessary and unimportant distractions. God's Word will provide the insight that we need not only to succeed, but to choose the successes that matter.

Excellence Awaits

In the chapters to come we will be covering the behaviors of successful communications—how to get confidence in a practical way and use it with the power of visual impact. You will undoubtedly discover that this knowledge and practicing these behaviors will raise your skill levels and provide you a key to success in many areas of relationships and life. But the firepower for excellence does not come from the skill sets—it comes from God's indwelling Spirit of power, love, and self-discipline, and then striving and reaching for what God wants us to do.

It is exciting to know that if we just trust in God's power and desire to be used by him to reach the world around us, excellence—as well as success—awaits us. Imagine what your life and impact can be if you can learn to convey God's truth to those you know. You will see success in your marriage, your parenting, your job, and your ministry. Whether witnessing to a friend, talking to your teenager about drugs, or teaching a Bible study class, you will see results because through God's Word you have learned the secret of letting others see your heart, not just hear your facts.

High-Level Excellence

There is one more avenue to achieving high-level excellence and competence. One of the most important things Jesus said to his disciples as he sent them out to preach in the surrounding towns was, ". . . 'be as shrewd as snakes and as innocent as doves'" (Matt. 10:16). Christians tend to veer toward the innocent-as-doves side. Many of us are filled with love and grace, so much so that we often excuse mediocrity or downright incompetence in the name of "love." And we remain silent, afraid to confront any lack of excellence in effort. Jesus never did that. He was filled with grace and love, but he was also filled with a standard of excellence that he held up to others, and it's captured in his phrase to the disciples.

Be as effective as you can be in your world and in your marketplace. You are dealing with others who are perhaps only thinking of effectiveness and competence and don't have any of the grace and love that you have, and you have to be able to deal with them. You must be shrewd as snakes in your discernment, in your level of competence and effectiveness, and in efficiently shining your light on the world.

Success Begins with Commitment

You have a desire to succeed or you wouldn't be reading this book. Something tells you that you need to improve your ability to communicate to others. Ironically, that outreach to others has to flow from your commitment to not only these principles, but to the Lord himself. The only way you will inspire them is if they see inspiration in you. And that passion, that success, begins with the process described in Proverbs 16:3: "Commit to the LORD whatever you do, and your plans will succeed."

If you have not already done so, pause right now and commit your communication efforts to God. Ask him for his wisdom, for his direction, and even for his desires. And as you surrender your abilities, your desires, your fears, and your time to him in pursuit of the excellence he deserves, you will take an important step toward experiencing the bold assurance that is available to you.

Part II
The Basis of Bold Assurance

OK, you are convinced that you need to be a better communicator. You probably even have some specific situations that you want to address. You don't need to be further convinced or convicted. You just want to know *how* to change. Maybe you aren't looking for a magic wand to wave and have instant communicative success, but you *do* want to know the steps you can follow that lead to improvement and success.

You are probably expecting us to say something like, "Sorry, but it's not that simple," but you aren't going to find that here. To the contrary, we believe it really *is* that simple. Being a better communicator is not as hard as you might imagine. It just requires an open mind, a willing spirit, a ready heart, and the discipline to apply these principles in your daily life.

In the following chapters, you are going to learn the secret of powerful and effective communication that positively impacts those you want to influence. You will begin to understand more about all the tools you have at your disposal that you can use to earn trust and reach your audience, whether you are speaking to your spouse, a sales meeting, a Bible study class, or preaching to an audience of hundreds. But first, you must shed some myths that may have crept into your mind and belief system.

CHAPTER 5
The Three Myths of Communicating

"The truth will set you free." Oh, really? Many quote that verse—partially—as we just did, and miss its power and impact. What Jesus actually said in John 8:32 was, "'Then you will *know* the truth, and the truth will set you free'" (emphasis added). In other words, incorrect belief and ignorance of God's truth, even about communicating, will keep you imprisoned and deprived of the impact and power that God desires for you.

There are three communication myths that are crippling if we believe them, and must be displaced by the truth if we are to reach our full potential. These myths rob you of effective connection with others, so it's important that you understand why each of the myths is incorrect and rid your mind of these debilitating thieves of effectiveness.

Myth #1: "But I'm not a public speaker!"

What do you envision when you think of public speaking? Do you see someone behind a lectern giving a programmed speech—perhaps a preacher, an executive, or a politician? That's the mental image most of us have, but it is a tiny part of public speaking. In truth, you don't have to fit into one of these categories to be a public speaker, because unless you live in isolation or are mute, you *are* a public speaker. Virtually all of your speech is public to someone! In other words, you have an audience whether it consists of one person on the phone, a group at a meeting, or the more formal setting of hundreds or thousands in an audience. These are all public speaking. So replace the myth with *Truth #1: "I am a public speaker!"*

Certainly there are appropriate times for self-talk, talking with God, even "groans that words cannot express" when the Holy Spirit has to pray for us (Rom. 8:26). But the vast majority of our spoken communication is public, whether at home, on the job, in a class, or at the grocery. If you speak more to yourself than you do to others, you probably aren't shaping your world as much as you could—and in God's eyes—as much as you should!

If so much of our time is spent in public speaking, then we need to learn how to do it more effectively. Few things that you study will be as rewarding or even as enjoyable as learning the art of communicating with others. And few things will help you accomplish God's will in your life like meaningful communication.

What did the apostle Paul mean when he wrote that our speech should always be "seasoned with salt"? Not only does salt flavor and enhance, but salt has a wonderful preservative power that our ancestors knew well. Before the luxury of electricity and refrigeration, meat, fish, and other perishable items were salted and kept for a long time. But in order for that salt to work, it had to be applied.

So it is with the wonderful gift of speech. With all of its tremendous power to motivate, instruct, and change lives, our speech does no good unless we use it. In even the most intimate family situations, our speech has incredible potential to affect the world. "Through patience a ruler can be persuaded, and a gentle tongue can break a bone" (Prov. 25:15). With a word we can encourage or devastate, edify or destroy, help or hinder.

Myth #2: "If I just say the words, people will get it."

We have been taught that if we just say the right words, people will get our message. Our academic system teaches us to respect only the intellect and mind that creates the words, and we are taught, by omission, to ignore the delivery system—the voice and body that impart life to the words. Replace this myth with the reality of *Truth #2: "Speaking uses the mind and body."* Speaking uses the whole self, not just the intellect and the mind.

Imagine that it is 1940, and you live in England. Weakened by the Depression and your former government's mindless treaty with Hitler, you are totally unprepared when Nazi guns turn their sights on your country. You wonder how your nation will survive the newly declared war. Full of anxiety and worry, you turn on the radio. The new prime minister, Sir Winston Churchill, is speaking. In a dull monotonous voice, with no hint of emotion, let alone passion, he reads the text of his speech. "This is (yawn) England's, uh, finest, um, hour." And with no more fervor or conviction than that, the leader of the nation drones on for an hour, laying out the plans for the defense of the nation. "We will fight, ahhh, in the, ahem, fields. We will fight on the (pause) beaches."

You are hardly comforted, are you? Why? Because you need more than your intellect engaged! And few knew that better than Winston Churchill. Unlike the imaginary example above, his speeches relied on passion and fire, not just words and phrases.

Do not misunderstand. We are not saying that the intellect can be ignored, that it is unimportant, or that it does not matter. Certainly it matters, but great communicators do not appeal solely to the intellect. Can you think of great speeches, whether spiritual or otherwise, that you have heard? If you just read the printed text of those speeches, would they have an equal impact? Would Martin Luther King's "I Have a Dream" speech be as memorable if you just read it? Would Franklin Roosevelt's fireside chats have kept a nation going if they had only appeared in newspapers?

If you compare great speeches, talks, and sermons you have heard, the common denominator is the emotional impact that they made, the way they made you feel. That is what you remember. You don't remember the content; you remember the *connection,* how they stirred you, moved you. That connection made you happy, angry, sad, thankful. It made you want to do something.

We all know this intuitively. We have experienced it every time someone has really touched us. So why do we insist that speaking is an intellectual process? It has intellectual *content,* but when it is effective, it uses a conduit of emotion that reveals the heart, not just the head.

No one understood and used this principle better than Jesus. He did not just tell an audience that God wants the lost found; he told a story about a shepherd who lost one sheep, a woman who lost one coin, and a father who lost one son. He made the emotional connection with a story so the intellectual content would be *felt* as well as comprehended. He could have just said something like, "God wants us to look for the lost," but he chose a better and more memorable route. He connected with the emotions first. He helped his listeners identify with the concept personally so that they could comprehend and apply the truth.

One of the greatest mistakes would-be communicators make is that they put all of their efforts into *content*—reaching the head—and none into passion—reaching the heart. The Sunday school teacher who simply reads the material, the pastor who gets bogged down in cultural detail, the salesperson who recites facts and figures—each of these misses the real target of the spoken word. We have to reach listeners' hearts before we reach their minds.

Myth #3: "Writing speeches works."

The spoken medium is actually entirely different from the written word. That is why we don't recommend writing out sermons, presentations, and speeches and then reading them, even though this is traditionally accepted practice. There is a better way, and the most effective communicators use it. In later chapters we will fully develop a process that will guarantee that you never have to write out a sermon or speech again—at least in text and manuscript form. And you will be more effective in your delivery and be able to create your presentation in perhaps half the time. Replace this wasteful and ineffective myth with *Truth #3: "Speaking is not writing."*

Actually, few business presentations, sermons, Bible study lessons, or speeches fail because of a lack of proper content. Conscientious people normally work hard to prepare the right material. They know the information they want to communicate, and so they think that if they craft their words carefully and clearly their listeners will be so impressed and caught up in their skillful presentation that they will really "get it."

When it comes to *giving* a talk, we work hard to get just the right word, to turn just the right phrase, believing all the while that our hard work as a wordsmith will be rewarded by an audience that will listen and be gratefully impressed that we have elevated the intellect. Our experience as a *listener*, however, tells us the truth—that the greatest message can be undermined by a less-than-exciting messenger. Everyone can recall sleeping through a speech or a sermon that was unquestionably true, important, and even needed, but it didn't matter—because we were bored, sleepy, daydreaming, or just unconcerned. A lack of energy, passion, and conviction in the speaker's voice and manner—even though his speech was skillfully prepared and represented hours of labor—puts us to sleep.

Hershael:

I will never forget the first time I heard David preach in my class. When he finished, I told him, "You preach like a writer," and I did not mean that as a compliment. I found no fault in his treatment of the biblical passage he had chosen for his text. He was faithful to its meaning and explained it and applied it very well. He was quite an eloquent wordsmith as well. His care in choosing just the right word and diction was obvious.

The problem was that he paid so much attention to his masterpiece manuscript that he almost forgot that he had an audience. He read it verbatim, hardly glancing at the room full of listeners. He cared so much about the perfect words and content that he failed to notice whether anyone cared.

When I explained to him what he had done, I issued a challenge. "The next time you preach, I want you to take a big risk," I said. "I want you to quit caring so much about just the right word and instead I want you to be moved by your belief in what you are saying, your conviction that your audience desperately needs what you have to give them. Step away from the lectern and your manuscript, look into the eyes of your congregation, and let them see your heart."

I admit that I had only moderate expectations of improvement the next time it was David's turn to preach. After all, I had given the same advice to scores of other seminarians that semester, and few of them had really been willing to take the kind of risk I was talking about.

As soon as David began, however, I saw that there had been a seismic shift in his approach. He began with a story about the best prayer he had ever heard. It came from the lips of a little boy in an orphanage where he had worked. Soon he was preaching from the Lord's Prayer, a well-known but difficult passage to preach. He hardly ever glanced at his notes. He was, instead, moved with a passion and a zeal about the simplicity of prayer and how God hears it. He interjected personal stories that engaged and amused us. He was intensely personal, yet right on target with his passage.

When he finished, I could not speak. I, like much of the class, was in tears. It felt almost profane to issue a grade to such a holy and heartfelt sermon, even though it was given in a classroom. Was his content better than the first sermon? Only marginally. What made the difference—one that still lingers with me years later—was the *emotional connection* he made, not from writing a speech, but from touching a heart.

In truth, writing speeches does not work because it does not account for the striking difference between written communication and spoken communication. Written communication can be very effective, but it relies on a command of the language, a knowledge of the subject, an appropriate style. Written communication is most effective for giving straight information, and when you need to refer to facts and figures. But when you want to create action and persuade, that's when you want to speak it. Spoken communication has many more tools at the disposal of the one using it. Speech incorporates all the tools of the written word and then adds an almost infinite number of nuances and variations that reach people on the feeling level.

Take, for instance, the simple sentence "I never said you stole that car." It is quite a simple sentence, but on this page its meaning is limited just to the words used and to the experience, mood, and predisposition of the reader. Now, imagine someone saying those words. How does the meaning differ if the speaker slouches while he says the sentence? What if he raises an eyebrow? What if he winks? Speaks rapidly? Points to a toy car? Imagine that he repeats the sentence seven times, but each time he emphasizes a different word.

"*I* never said you stole that car."
"I *never* said you stole that car."
"I never *said* you stole that car."
"I never said *you* stole that car."
"I never said you *stole* that car."
"I never said you stole *that* car."
"I never said you stole that *car.*"

In each case, as you picture the speaker and hear his voice in your imagination, you get a different meaning, nuance, or implication.

Now imagine that, along with the vocal emphasis on the word "never," the speaker is looking at you menacingly, with his eyes furrowed, his brow wrinkled, and his fist clenched. Or picture that while he emphasizes the word "never" he is crying, his hands outstretched to you. Do you begin to see the infinite number of possibilities as you combine the words with such physical variations as eye movements, hand gestures, a smile or a frown, or posture? Written communication is limited to the words on a page, but speech is accompanied by a veritable workshop of tools.

That is why oral communication is almost always the most effective kind of interaction. So we need to pay attention not only to the words we say, but to the behaviors that conduct our message to our hearers.

CHAPTER 6
Behavior

We evaluate credibility—whether we will *trust* someone or not—on much more than just words. On a subconscious level, we are constantly processing all kinds of visual and verbal clues whenever we communicate with someone.

Our behavior is the conduit that conveys the content of our speech. In other words, you might have the most thrilling, exciting news in the world as the content of your speech, but if your behavior conveys anything less than that—if you send a mixed signal—you will not only confuse your listeners, *you will lose them.*

Imagine a preacher smiling as he preaches on the horrors of eternal punishment. Wouldn't that make you feel strange and uncomfortable? The mixed signal makes you question his credibility or, worse yet, his qualifications.

Conversely, imagine as you share the gospel—the most exciting, life-changing story in history—that you seem unmoved, you sound monotone, and no smile or hint of excitement crosses your face. You even look at your watch repeatedly while you share the good news. Do you really expect your friend to want a relationship with Christ that has aroused no passion in you?

Though only God can apply his truth to a person's life, *you* are responsible to get your message to her ear. She will not give an honest and thoughtful hearing to a message that is incongruent with everything else she sees in your expression, posture, and body language.

We do not mean to imply that you will always get the results you want or that your magnetism and charm can sway everyone. Learning effective communication does not mean that people will always do whatever you want them to do. It means that you send a *clear message* that they can hear and appreciate without being distracted by any behavior that makes them question the reliability of that message.

Used car salesmen are notorious! A frequent butt of jokes, they have an image as dishonest, opportunistic shysters who will try to sell a lousy car at an exorbitant price. That is why Joe *loves* being a used car salesman. He gets to shatter the stereotype. Because he is a believer, he genuinely wants to see people buy a car that they will enjoy for a long time—and at a fair price. He goes for the double win.

So Joe makes certain that everything he does breeds confidence in his clients. Instead of flashy clothes, he goes for the "country-club casual" look. He talks to customers about their lives, not just the cars they own. He laughs easily, smiles genuinely, and speaks distinctly. He treats every customer as if he were selling a car to his parents—and it shows. Not only are his sales high, but his customers come back *and* recommend him to their friends. Joe doesn't get every customer that comes his way, but he loses *none* because of a lack of trust. Everything about him breeds confidence.

SKILLS

The exciting part of all this is that once you know these powerful liberating concepts, you can become a potent and effective communicator, whether in someone's living room or in an auditorium filled to capacity. All you have to do is understand, practice, and master *nine communication skills.* In other words, God has given you nine powerful tools you can use to get his message of truth and love across to others. To master these nine skills is to master communication. You are in control of these things all the time if only you will consciously use them to your advantage in order to get your message across. Once you *know* them, you must discipline yourself to *use* them. There is no mystery to them—in fact, they seem deceptively simple—so we will introduce them to you now. In the next chapters we will explore them in depth so you will see that they are simple, common sense skills that are very powerful. They are:

- *Eye communication:* the ability to make and maintain eye contact in a meaningful way.
- *Gestures and facial expression:* animation communicated through your face and body that corresponds with your message and conveys energy.

- *Posture and movement:* reflecting confidence and energy in your body position and movement.
- *Dress and appearance:* presenting yourself in a way that does not detract from the message you want your hearer to grasp.
- *Voice and vocal variety:* employing pitch, volume, and vocal energy that will keep your listener engaged in the content of what you are saying.
- *Words and fillers:* using language that is replete with meaning, effective pauses, and devoid of "fillers"—those annoying "ums" and "ahs" and meaningless phrases such as "whatever," "you know," "like," and "I mean."
- *Humor:* a healthy sense of humor about yourself and life in general that makes you approachable and likable.
- *Listener involvement:* simple ways to involve yourself with your listeners—whether one or one thousand—in order to help them listen.
- *The "Natural Self":* using these communication parameters to let the real you come through without seeming stiff or phony.

In part IV we will go into detail on each of these skills, giving you the concepts, examples, and exercises to gain mastery of each of them.

CHAPTER 7
The Listener-Based Message

Successful fishermen share a secret. No ordinary secret, this powerful ability enables them to catch fish when others do not. This truth separates the fisherman from the person who just gets a line wet. Do you know what that mysterious knowledge is?

The great fishermen know you must *think* like a fish.

Successful fishermen learn when and where fish will feed, what spooks them, what interests them, what excites them, what motion and colors attract them. Consequently, they select and use bait that appeals to the instincts of the fish they want to hook. Wouldn't it be ridiculous to choose bait based on its appeal to the fisherman?

What we have called a secret is really no secret at all. Advertisers, sales professionals, charitable organizations, and politicians do the same thing. They appeal to the way people think in order to sell their product, to land a donor, or to motivate a voter to get to the polls and cast a vote.

JESUS' METHODOLOGY

Christians have the most powerful message in the world. We know that the gospel is the world's greatest need and only hope. We are convinced that it is God's power that leads to salvation, but in our commitment to the power of that message, we often lose sight of the fact that our listeners first have to be shown *why* they need it. We can be so convinced of its ultimate impact that we assume the listeners share our interest, which causes us to present our ideas poorly.

Jesus never made that mistake though. The third chapter of John records Jesus' encounter with Nicodemus, a biblical expert of Jesus' time. Jesus even complimented him by calling Nicodemus "Israel's teacher." But when Christ spoke to him, he met him on his level. Nicodemus was a theologian, so Jesus talked to him about theology. Jesus said the things that would "hook" Nicodemus and get his attention, challenge him to think and to examine the way he thought about Jesus.

But the next chapter of John is different. In John 4 Jesus is not dealing with a theologian, but an immoral, outcast Samaritan woman. Rather than coming to the well early in the morning to draw water with the other women, as was customary, she came in the middle of the day, probably because the other women would have nothing to do with her. Finding her there, Jesus began to talk to her about the one thing that was immediately on her mind and in her plan—water. He asked her for a drink and then told her that if she knew who he was, she would ask *him* for a drink. Using the metaphor of water to tell her about his identity as the Water of Life, Jesus helped her repent of her sins and accept him as her Messiah.

These two scenes from the life of Christ demonstrate that though his message of repentance and the new birth did not change, his method of telling someone this life-changing word purposely changed. What was the common denominator? His message was *listener-based.* In other words, Jesus told his message in such a way that his audience, even an audience of one, could relate and understand what he was saying. He met his listeners where they were, not where he wanted them to be or where he thought they should have been. He tailored his message—in style if not in substance—to their life situations and to their experiences.

PAUL'S METHODOLOGY

The apostle Paul knew his audience too. His usual policy was to take the gospel to the Jew first, and so in every town he entered he would first seek the local Jewish synagogue. While worshiping there, he would tell his Jewish audience that Jesus was the Messiah, the Christ, because he fulfilled the prophecies of the Scriptures. Jews were familiar with the messianic prophecies and were predisposed to hear the story of Jesus, so Paul took full advantage of that.

When he went to a Gentile audience, however, it was different. He used their own preconceptions and understanding as an entry point for the gospel. Acts 17 records Paul's sermon on the Areopagus, the Athenian court and seat of government. He began his presentation of the gospel with a reference to the Greeks' pagan religion, explaining to them that God is the "Unknown God" that they had blindly worshiped, but that the real way to worship him is through his Son, Jesus. For them his message was not primarily that Jesus fulfilled Old Testament prophecy, for they did not even know what that was. Rather, Paul focused on Jesus as God come to earth to pay for their sins and to remove their guilt.

Paul even gave guidance to us in the Bible when he said,

> I make myself a slave to everyone, to win as many as possible. To the Jews I became like a Jew, to win the Jews. To those under the law I became like one under the law (though I myself am not under the law), so as to win those under the law. To those not having the law I became like one not having the law (though I am not free from God's law but am under Christ's law), so as to win those not having the law. To the weak I became weak, to win the weak. I have become all things to all men so that by all possible means I might save some. (1 Cor. 9:19–22)

KNOWING OUR AUDIENCE

Too many times Christian speakers are so confident of their message that they lose sight of their audience. Certainly our *message* is powerful and divine. After all, this is God's story. The Word of God does not need to be nor should it be altered in any way. Yet we must make no apology for striving to change our *method*, the way we present that message, to make it comprehensible and attractive to an audience.

HOW TO ADAPT TO LISTENERS

Whenever we wish to convey some truth, we do so from a particular *point of view*. This is our own perspective that motivates us to speak, to share what we know. If we share the gospel, for instance, our point of view is that this message truly transforms lives. It is the only hope of salvation for our listener, and it can provide forgiveness and peace with God in this life and in the next. But if we stop at our point of view, we are thinking only of ourselves. If we just walk up to someone and tell her our point of view, she probably won't respond favorably. If *our* perspective were all that mattered, we would be convinced we got our message across, but it is unlikely we would convince our listeners.

We must think of our listener or audience as well. We ask a simple question: Who are our *listeners*? If we are preaching or leading a Bible study, do our listeners even know who God is? It hardly makes sense to tell them that

Jesus is God's Son if they do not know there is a God. Do they have any concept of the Bible? Quoting Scripture will have little impact if they don't believe it to begin with. It makes no sense to ask them if they are going to heaven if they don't believe heaven exists. Once we know who our listeners are, we can tailor the way we present the message to them.

In part V we will give you a complete methodology for making sure that your message reaches your listeners. You will learn how to organize your presentations around four basic cornerstones:

1. Point of View. What is your stance, attitude, or opinion about the subject?
2. Listeners. What are their needs and their attitudes about the subject and about you?
3. Action Steps. What do you want your listeners to do?
4. Benefits. How will your listeners benefit by taking the steps you are urging?

From these cornerstones of the listener-based message you will learn a patented grid system that will enable you to create, organize, and compose messages of any length without writing them out—and in half the time.

A listener-based message considers matters of culture, experience, and education. It might be as obvious as speaking to children on their own level, or it might be more complex, like understanding how a person in a particular culture thinks. This is the key to cross-cultural communication, such as missionaries must learn; cross-generational connection, such as a youth minister needs to employ; and sharing our faith in a way that really connects with a listener. Most sermons, speeches, and testimonies are written out and given from the perspective of the giver. But we should focus on the listener.

Jesus gathered a bunch of fishermen and turned them into fishers of men. Do you want to catch fish too? Then think like a fish.

Part III
What Counts in Communicating

What is the most important thing in communicating? Is it substance or style? Is it content or delivery? Simply put, it's *both*. You cannot effectively have one without the other. If you divorce them from one another, you will fail to be the communicator God wants you to be.

There are basically three kinds of communicators. The first is the "great" communicator who really doesn't say much. He is all flash and no substance. He engages his audience, using humor and making an emotional connection. Time passes swiftly as he tells stories, puts his audience at ease, and makes them feel at home with his personal style. But when he is finished, you aren't really sure what his point was. Like eating cotton candy, you leave feeling like you enjoyed him, but on reflection you realize that you took nothing of substance away with you.

The second kind of communicator is the person who has great content, but you really didn't get it because she put you to sleep. She was very educated about her topic. In fact, she told you more about it than you ever wanted to know, but you got lost in the statistics, the technical information, and the monotony. You didn't doubt that her information was correct, even important, but you just didn't get it all because your attention waned. She just didn't hold your interest. Like eating broccoli, you know you need it—it's good for you—but you really don't look forward to it.

Then there is the kind of communicator that we aspire to be—who has something important to say and says it well. We strive to know what to say and how to connect with people or an audience so they get it and embrace it. When we have life-changing information, our countenance, posture, expression, and energy all tell listeners that what we have to say is worthwhile, that it has changed our lives too. We strive for nutrition *and* taste.

According to the New Testament, people stood for hours listening to Jesus, even going hungry while his impassioned words enthralled and challenged them. Did they do it only because TV hadn't yet shortened their attention spans? Or was it because everything about Jesus communicated that he could be trusted and that his message was what they desperately needed?

The balance between content and delivery, between style and substance, is probably not what you have been taught or what you might think. And knowing that balance can transform your communication. In this section you will learn that building trust in your listener is critical and is based on some surprising fundamentals. By learning how to build credibility and gain the trust of your audience you are giving weight and significance to the life-changing message of truth that it deserves.

CHAPTER 8
Building Trust in the Messenger

What makes us respond to a fund-raising appeal? What makes us hear a sermon? Why does the advice some people offer make us appreciate them, while the same advice given by others makes us mad? What is the magic ingredient that makes a person's message compelling? Why do we intuitively receive and believe some people, while we mistrust others?

TRUST IS THE KEY

Everyone wants to be believed, but unfortunately we share the planet with a lot of dishonest and unscrupulous characters. It is natural and healthy to take much of what we hear with a grain of salt, to have a healthy degree of skepticism. Though we all listen that way, we hate to be heard that way. We don't want to think that anyone questions our sincerity, our intention, or even our information. We want to be *trusted*.

And make no mistake about it: trust is the most critical element in communication. You've got to be believed to be heard. No one will care what your message is if they don't trust you. In fact, your audience, whether it be of one or one thousand, rarely hears your message if something in your behavior makes your listeners think, even on a subconscious level, that you are not trustworthy.

If we want our message to be heard and accepted, then we must do everything possible to gain trust. If we are doing anything that unwittingly undermines our message, we must ruthlessly eliminate that behavior. Everything about our expression, demeanor, posture, tone, and attitude must demonstrate that we are sincere and passionate about our message.

So how do we do that?

The Importance of Behavior

Do you remember the list of nine behaviors from chapter 6? The reason these make speakers so effective is that they are the great credibility builders. These are the behaviors that tell an audience, even on a subconscious level, that the speaker is trustworthy. Here are the nine behavioral skills that have such an impact on our communications that we will explore in depth in the next few chapters: eye communication, gestures and facial expression, posture and movement, dress and appearance, voice and vocal variety, words and fillers, humor, listener involvement, the "natural self."

If our behavior lacks these communication skills, we inadvertently invite our listeners to doubt our word. In essence, we send a mixed signal. Our words say, "Believe me," but our behavior triggers doubt.

No matter how skillful our words, how profound our truth, how artistic our presentation, we must never forget that we *are* the message. They won't hear us if our behavior gets in the way. Conversely, if we distract with behavior that is obtrusive, they see us, but not our message.

Sending a Mixed Message

When we carry a positive message but we have a negative behavior, our listeners are confused. When a husband tells his wife that he loves her, but he leers at other women, he sends a mixed message. When a pastor is listening to a parishioner's hurts, but he glances at his watch, he is really saying that he has something else that is more important. When a Christian looks grim as he shares the gospel, he is hardly making that lost person feel that Christianity is something that he wants.

When we send a mixed message, saying one thing with our words but another with our actions, which one do you think has the greatest impact?

A spoken message is made up of only three components: the *verbal*, the *vocal*, and the *visual*. Several years ago, Professor Albert Mehrabian of UCLA conducted a landmark study on the relationships between these three *V*s of spoken communication. He measured the effect that each of these three components has on the believability of our message.

The verbal element is the message itself—the words you say. Most of us tend to concentrate *only* on the verbal element, mistakenly assuming this to be *the* message, when in fact it is only *part* of the message. The second part of the message is the vocal element—the intonation, projection, and resonance of your voice as it carries the words. And the third part is the visual element—what people see—the motion and expression of your body and face as you speak.

Let's do an experiment. Think for a moment about how these three elements of your spoken message—verbal, vocal, and visual—work together to reach and persuade your listener. In the chart below write your estimate of the percentage of impact each element has on the believability of your message. If you think the verbal part of the message accounts for 50 percent of a person's determination of believability, then write that. Or maybe 25/25/50 percent. Or if you think they are all equal, write $33^1/3$ percent for each. Make sure that your percentages add up to one hundred percent.

> ## What Counts: *Believability*
>
> Verbal _____
>
> Vocal _____
>
> Visual _____
>
> Total **100%**

Write them down, and when you are finished, you can compare your answers to what Mehrabian's studies determined—on the next page. We think you will be quite surprised at what you thought and what the research has shown. For the truth of the relationships between these three communication components is not the way we are taught communications in school—or in seminaries, the business world, or life, for that matter.

(Make sure you have written your answers before you turn the page to get the full impact of this important finding.)

In his research, Albert Mehrabian found that when we send out an inconsistent message, our verbal content is virtually smothered by the vocal and visual components. Just look at his results:

What Counts: *Believability*	
Verbal	7%
Vocal	38%
Visual	55%
Total	**100%**

How did Mehrabian's actual results compare with your estimate on the previous page? Surprised? Yet it's absolutely true! When the vocal and visual components of our message are inconsistent with the verbal content of our message, we will not be believed.

Don't misunderstand these statistics. This does not mean that a listener gets only seven percent of a speaker's verbal content or that ninety-three percent of the listener's judgment of a speaker is based on body language. What Professor Mehrabian found is that these percentages are valid when there is an inconsistent message. In other words, if your demeanor matches the content of what you say, your audience is free to more carefully listen to actual content and to judge rationally. But when listeners see and hear a discrepancy between what you say and how you are saying it, the manner of your speech and behavior carries the overwhelmingly major impact.

When we learn how to coordinate all three of these components to form one totally consistent message, we are not only believable, *we have impact.* The excitement and enthusiasm of your voice work with the energy and animation of your face and body to reflect the conviction of your message.

When your words, your voice, and your delivery are all working in harmony, your message dynamically and persuasively reaches your listener, having the fully intended impact.

On the other hand, when you appear nervous, awkward, or under pressure, your verbal content is blocked by your inconsistent vocal and visual message. For example, when someone says, "I'm happy to be here," but looks at the floor, talking in a halting, tremulous voice, clasping his hands together in front of his body in an edgy, inhibited "fig-leaf" position, he is sending an inconsistent message. His words will not be trusted, because the visual channel dominates what is believed.

What does the visual channel tell the listener about us when we send out an inconsistent message? Perhaps it says we are insincere or lacking in confidence, or that we have something to hide. Perhaps it just conveys to the listener a feeling of anxiety or boredom.

WYSIWYG is a computer term that stands for "What you see is what you get." It applies to personal impact as well. The message you *see* is the message you *get*. Clearly, the primary path to believability is through the visual channel.

Making It Work

Now that you know this powerful reality, you must put it to work for you and, most importantly, for those you want to impact. Do you want your children to know that you love them? You might look them in the eye when you say it, get down on a knee to talk to a three-year-old, pause, and pay attention. Do you want your Bible study class to really get the life-changing power of the Bible? Then your energy and excitement when you teach must convey the excitement and power that you have discovered. Do you want to lead your coworker to Christ, even though you know he has a low opinion of Christianity and most Christians? Then you must learn to convey nonjudgmental love and concern in the way you speak to him, especially when you share the gospel.

Do you want your audience to believe your message? Then first you must get them to believe *you*.

CHAPTER 9

The Victory of the Visual

Some people find these concepts of communication difficult to accept. For years they have spent so much time in getting the facts, in organizing a lesson or a talk, in planning *what* to say, that they have hardly thought at all about *how* to say it. They recoil at the thought that they could have invested so much for so little return.

But that is precisely what we do. Like it or not, God has made us visual creatures. Pastors don't mail printed texts of their sermons to parishioners, they deliver them in person. Philips Brooks, the great preacher of the nineteenth century, knew this when, in his Yale lectures on preaching, he defined preaching as "truth through personality." And more than anything else, personality, that part of us that really convinces our audience of our own commitment, is revealed *visually*. In other words, they consciously and subconsciously are looking for clues to whether they can trust our message or not.

Have you ever stopped to ask directions? Imagine that you are in a strange city and that you cannot find where you need to go. After much frustration and futility, you pull over to a convenience store to ask a local citizen how you can get to your destination.

As you get out of the car, you immediately see about twenty people standing around. Whom do you ask? Do you ask the man in cowboy boots with the cigar who seems to be pointing at you and laughing? Do you ask the young mother who is frustrated with her toddler and is yanking his arm in fury? Do you ask the teenagers who seem oblivious to you? Or do you ask the middle-aged gentleman who has a pleasant smile and whose eyebrows are raised in expectation? Your mind immediately and subconsciously processes every clue and nuance of posture, expression, demeanor, and even dress to see who you should trust.

But the big news is this: every time you speak, that is exactly how others are subconsciously evaluating *you*. Can they trust you? Should they believe you? Are you really convinced of what you are saying to them?

We've used the term WYSIWYG, which stands for "What you see is what you get." Good communicators understand that listeners get what they see. If they see nervousness, even if the speaker is giving a talk on "Ten Reasons Why Worry Is a Sin," they will get a very different message than the one the speaker intended.

Why is the visual element so important in communication? Why must we come to the inescapable conclusion that we must give attention to the way we behave as we speak? Put simply, because that is the way God made us.

God's Glorious Design

The visual is very, very powerful. The nerve pathways of the eye to the brain are twenty-five times larger than the nerve pathways from the ear to the brain. The eye is the only sensory organ that contains brain cells. Memory improvement experts invariably emphasize techniques that link the information you want to remember to a *visual* image. Over the past few years a huge body of research has been amassed, demonstrating that of all the sensory input the brain registers, it is the visual input that makes the greatest impact. Clearly, the *visual* sense dominates *all* of the senses.

God made us very sensitive creatures. During those periods of human history when survival was threatened almost daily, we had to pick up on subtle nuances. Our very lives depend on our ability to differentiate between a threat and a haven.

Oh, Be Careful Little Eyes What You See

Why does the visual sense dominate? According to scientific estimates, the nerve endings of our eyes are struck by seven hundred thousand stimuli every instant. We cannot escape the massive impact of this bombardment on our brain. Psychologists have said that viewing something three times has the power of one actual experience. This fact alone has enormous consequence in our movie and TV habits and in how we use our powers of visualization. This has no doubt contributed to recent rashes of school violence.

Consider the impact of viewing *The Texas Chainsaw Massacre* or a pornographic movie three times. The destructive impact of seeing those scenes portrayed three times would be similar to seeing the actual event just once. The power of vision can be used for good or ill. But there is no question that it is a strong, strong power.

Television has exaggerated this natural phenomenon of visual dominance in this age. Most of today's adults were raised on television, and are much more visually sophisticated than their parents. Television is used as a convenient baby-sitter so that today's children will probably be even more visually oriented. The subtleties of a glance or a coy smile are significant—and they communicate. Such nuances weren't as critical in previous times.

Once you understand the significance of the visual and how it is exaggerated today, you begin to appreciate both the power and the responsibility of communication. The visual element of communication often determines whether or not listeners hear the content of our message.

GETTING PAST THE GATEKEEPER

Effective communication is a lot more than simply transferring information. Every time you hear someone speak or teach, there is a gateway to your mind through which communication must pass. Standing guard before the house of your rational mind is a gatekeeper. This gatekeeper makes a quick assessment of the messenger to determine whether he will let the information pass into the intellect. We call this gatekeeper the *feeling brain*. Will the gatekeeper open or close the gate of communication? Will the message get through, or will it be blocked?

Whenever we communicate, our listener's gatekeeper is right there on guard, figuratively asking, "Friend or foe?" The gatekeeper has complete power to grant or deny access to our listener's higher analytical and decision-making processes. The best communicator is the person who knows how to befriend the gatekeeper, who knows how to become "feeling-brain friendly," so that his or her message can get through effectively and persuasively.

When it comes to communicating the Word of God, we know that no human can get the message from the ear to a person's heart. Only God can do that. But it is our job to get the message to the person's ear, and he won't really hear us unless we learn to get past the gatekeeper.

FEELING BRAIN FIRST

We literally have a brain within a brain. We tend to think of our cerebral cortex, the analytical thinking brain, as our entire brain, but there's more to it. Housed inside all that surface brain area that is the cerebral cortex is what we call the feeling brain, which is composed of the brain stem and the limbic system. The cerebral cortex, of which God gave the majority share to his human beings, is our rational side. The feeling brain contains the limbic system, which is our emotional brain, and the brain stem, which is our unconscious immediate response system. He gave this more primitive brain in more generous portion to the animals, but we have it as well and use it continuously since it's the seat of human emotion.

In the last several years, extensive new brain research techniques have enabled us to see that all of our sensory input—particularly seeing and hearing—go into the feeling brain areas before they are later analyzed by the thinking brain. The feeling brain is that nonrational gatekeeper that subconsciously takes in all visual and auditory cues and clues and decides whether to accept the information first, and then how to accept it.

To communicate effectively you *must* be aware of the language of the feeling brain and you must *use* it. The language of the feeling brain is mostly a *visual* language.

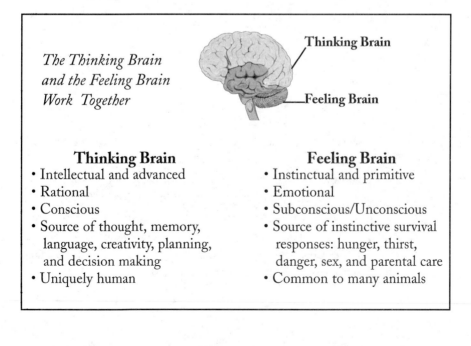

The Thinking Brain and the Feeling Brain Work Together

Thinking Brain

Feeling Brain

Thinking Brain
- Intellectual and advanced
- Rational
- Conscious
- Source of thought, memory, language, creativity, planning, and decision making
- Uniquely human

Feeling Brain
- Instinctual and primitive
- Emotional
- Subconscious/Unconscious
- Source of instinctive survival responses: hunger, thirst, danger, sex, and parental care
- Common to many animals

The Most Common Mistake

When most people speak, they think only of the rational part of the brain as their target. Bible study teachers think that if they just lay the facts out there, the class members will get it and their lives will be changed. Business executives believe that what is so obvious to them will be to others as well if they can only explain it rationally. Preachers assume that if they organize a sermon, if they just choose their words carefully, their parishioners will be moved to conviction and commitment.

Don't think for a moment that the rational part of the brain, that cognitive part that digests facts, evaluates data, and makes decisions is unimportant or uninvolved. To the contrary, that part of the brain is one of God's most marvelous gifts to mankind. But to reach that rational part of the brain our message must first pass through the feeling brain, the emotional part of the brain.

The Wellspring of Life

The wise author of the Proverbs wrote, "Above all else, guard your heart, for it is the wellspring of life" (Prov. 4:23). He recognized that the emotional part of a person is the key to that person's core existence. So the most important language in effective communication is the language of trust. In order to communicate effectively, we must make emotional contact with the listener. He must see that we are absolutely persuaded of what we are saying. And when he sees our passion and belief, he is more apt to really hear what we are saying.

Quite frankly, most people hate to admit that they are less than perfectly rational and deliberative people. We delude ourselves that we are never swayed by emotions, certainly not in the most important decisions of life. But that is not the way most people work, because that is not the way our minds work.

Salesmen have long known that *people buy on emotion and justify with fact*. No matter how much we resist that principle it remains true, and we can prove it. Think back to the major decisions you have made—your profession, your purchases of a house or car, or even choosing your spouse. These are major life-affecting decisions, and we all like to think we make such decisions in a fairly (if not completely) rational way.

But when you were making any of those big decisions, did you take out a yellow legal pad, write "Pro" and "Con" at the top, and make a list of all the reasons for deciding yes or no? When you chose your wife, did you make a list of her physical qualities, her prospects for income or child-bearing? Did you estimate her future maintenance costs based on the lifespan of her parents?

Even if we look at a decision like buying a house, you probably didn't make it purely on those practical reasons. Did you visit twenty houses and make a profile of every house you visited and compare and contrast the pros and cons? And if you actually did that, did you then make your choice purely on the basis of the weight of those answers? And what then were the primary, scale-tipping reasons for your decision? Even if you took those practical considerations into mind, your decision probably had more to do with how you felt in that house than any other factor. If the house was attractively presented, clean, and colorful, and you saw a breakfast nook that appealed to you or a playroom ideal for the children or a backyard with a little garden grove, these things probably swayed you. Then after you made a decision of the heart, you got your head involved and made sure that the facts supported the way you felt.

We aren't saying you didn't do research or give the decision a lot of thought. We are saying that most of our major decisions are overwhelmingly influenced at the emotional level, the subconscious level. We decide (or buy) at that level and then use our intellect to justify our decisions. Those emotions serve as the conduit to the intellect.

If you want to reach people's intellect, you must go through their heart, their emotions, their feeling brain first. Do you want that Bible study class to get excited about the principles you are teaching from the Sermon on the Mount? Do you want to convince that couple that the charity you work for is worth being included in their will? Then you must appear credible, excited, and make that emotional connection!

If we are energetic, enthusiastic, and believable, our words will actually be given more impact and energy by the listener's feeling brain before he is switched to the rational part of the brain. But if we appear boring, anxious, or insincere, our words will not even reach their destination. Instead, our message will be discolored or even tuned out at the switching station by our lack of believability. If we lack believability, we risk failure that has eternal consequences.

Use or Abuse?

Can these principles be abused? Certainly! Charlatans, manipulators, crooks, and politicians abuse them all the time! There are also unsavory characters who abuse food, sex, money, and talent. But food, sex, money, and talent are not evil, nor do they cause the problem. Those things can either be used to glorify God within their proper use and enjoyment, or they can be used to selfish and destructive ends.

And that is no less true with those who understand these powerful principles of communication. These principles are neither good nor bad. They just are! They reflect the way God made us. As with all knowledge, a great responsibility rests on the shoulders of those who understand. James knew that when he reminded us that teachers will be held to a high standard of judgment (James 3:1) and then explained the awesome power of the tongue.

Yet at the conclusion of that chapter, after warning of the destructive ability of the tongue, he wrote, "But the wisdom from above is first pure, then peaceable, gentle, reasonable, full of mercy and good fruits, unwavering, *without hypocrisy*" (James 3:17, NASB, emphasis added). What a description of the correct use of the tongue and communication principles!

Do We Sell the Gospel?

Please understand that the gospel is far more than something that we sell. No matter how persuasive or sincere we are, it still takes the work of the Holy Spirit and the grace of God to save a person. We are not at all suggesting that a person accepts the gospel based on the sophistication of our presentation. What we are suggesting is that he will not even *hear* the gospel if he does not find us credible. He must have an emotional response to *the evangelist* before he can ever hear *the evangel*. Though God can and does use many means to reach a person's heart, this has been his primary means for centuries.

Have you ever heard of someone being led to Christ by a person he thought was a liar or a cheat? Of course not! The one thing we have to contribute to the gospel is simply our belief, and *that* is what we want them to see.

Just think of the person whom God used to bring you to Christ. Was it someone you respected? Someone you trusted? Perhaps it was a chance encounter with someone you had never met, yet still there was something in her that told you that she had something worthwhile. You believed in *her*, so when she told you that the most important thing in life was the gospel of Jesus Christ, you were ready to listen.

That is why the greatest method of sharing the gospel is still personal evangelism. One on one, loving, intentional witnessing is our opportunity to be transparent and to let someone see what is at the very core of our being.

Hershael:

One of my pet peeves is the way movies and television portray Christians. In film, Christians are typically judgmental, unloving, duplicitous hypocrites who say one thing and do something else. Because of this popular portrayal, Christians should be doubly sensitive that everything about us—what we do, what we say, and how we say it—is being evaluated. Our message can't get through until we earn someone's confidence.

Never was that more apparent to me than when my wife and I entertained a successful writer whose lifestyle and outlook were very different from our own. During the evening we spent together, we talked openly and honestly about many differences that we had and about our desire to see him trust Christ and turn from his lifestyle, yet we developed a genuine affection and respect for one another. When the time came for him to leave, he told us that he hated to go because he had had such a good time. Then he said with great affection, "I've never met Christians like you." Those words both complimented and chilled me.

Authenticity is the ally we have.

FEELING-BRAIN FRIENDLY

How, then, do we make friends with the gatekeeper—the feeling brain—so that our message can get through the gate? How do we become feeling-brain friendly?

By being natural. By being truly authentic, which is being free from inhibition so we are just ourselves. By learning to use naturally the energy, enthusiasm, motion, expression—all the multichannel, nonverbal cues that God gave us to enable us to make emotional contact with the listener. By becoming looser and more spontaneous. By using all of those nine communication skills to give our message the credibility and impact that it deserves.

Many Christians know the *facts* of the Bible. Still many others know the *content* of the gospel. Why are some of them effective teachers, preachers, and witnesses and many others fail? Two people may have similar knowledge and education and each has a close walk with the Lord, yet one of them is more effective as a communicator. What makes the difference?

The great contrast is that—either intuitively or intentionally—effective communicators have learned how to become feeling-brain friendly. They know how to befriend the gatekeeper within their listeners, and thus they know how to get past the emotions so that the person *really* hears them.

CHAPTER 10

The Essence of Energy

Spoken communication is so much more powerful than the written word because it delivers on so many more channels. The written word is like a black-and-white still photograph, while spoken communication is high-definition color television!

Written words on a page communicate content well. Spoken words are better to create action. Spoken words carry more than just the face value of the words—they carry *passion*.

The written word tends to lie on the page, picked up by the passive but powerful eye. The spoken word captures the eye as well, but has to have energy behind it to stimulate the eye and reach the ear. Energy is a stimulus to the feeling brain. Whenever the feeling brain senses energy in communication, it swings the gate wide open. Important messages, messages that can even mean life or death, are usually delivered with great energy. Warnings of danger, the announcement of a birth, or a call to arms would be carried on waves of excitement and animation. Conversely, messages of relative unimportance almost always *lack* energy. No one gets excited about a comment about the weather—unless a tornado is on the way!

Imagine the impact this has on teaching, preaching, sharing the gospel, or coaching a Little League team! And imagine how ineffective you become when you ignore such a key.

Until the sixth grade, Paul was a marginal student, to put it kindly. Whenever papers were returned, Paul would dread looking at his because of all the red marks that were so obvious to every student in the classroom. He was the butt of their jokes, taunted for being dumb, and he just didn't fit.

Until the sixth grade. That is when Paul met Mrs. Southall. She *loved* teaching and *loved Paul*. He liked the way she smiled at him, the time she took with him, the encouragement she gave. And most of all, he loved to hear her teach. She always seemed so excited about the characters in the books they were reading. She was genuinely interested in what Paul thought too. Something in Mrs. Southall made Paul want to do better, made him want to learn, convinced him that he didn't have to be the worst student in class.

Today Paul has a doctorate degree in theology and is the director of a seminary. But what he likes to do most is teach, to let his passion ignite a smoldering spark in some student who wonders if she can do it. And if you ask him what made the difference, he will tell you that it was the enthusiasm of a teacher.

The enthusiasm and passion of a speaker is contagious. When you think of the great teachers you have had, you probably will remember most that they were excited about their subject. Their teaching style made it abundantly clear that they were passionate about their subject—they *loved* it. These examples, along with hundreds of others from politics and popular culture, remind us that our information is more caught than taught.

How to Be President

With the advent of television, American politics changed forever. Prior to television, candidates relied on newspaper, magazines, and other printed media to get their messages across in a complete and reasoned manner. Radio changed that slightly, adding the audio quality of the voice to the message, but nothing altered the process like the visual medium.

In the 1960 presidential election, almost universally seen as a watershed event, the upstart Kennedy campaign used the power of television like a club to pummel the opponent. Though Richard Nixon had the experience, the power, and platform of the vice-presidency, and an early lead in the polls, his campaign never understood the new medium of television. Not only did he fail to use it to his advantage, he allowed Kennedy to make him look foolish. During the now famous debates, Kennedy looked self-assured, confident, and in control. The heat of the lights made Nixon sweat uncomfortably. His brows were furrowed, and he came across as angry, mean, and less than the leader Americans wanted. In short, Kennedy looked more "presidential" and he was able to pull off the upset.

In every election since 1960 the American electorate has exhibited only one continuous trait: Americans elect the best communicator. No single party has dominated. Between 1960 and 2000, Democrats have been in the White House for twenty years as have Republicans. No clear ideology has emerged—except the ideology of passion and energy.

That does not mean that every president has been a great communicator, just that every president was a *better* communicator than his opponent. The lower the level of communication, the lower the excitement in the electorate.

Ronald Reagan, the "Great Communicator," was able to gather momentum and support by making Americans feel positive about America. After the quagmire of Vietnam, the betrayal of Watergate, the humiliation of the Iran hostage crisis, Reagan bounded onto the American stage with a lightness in his step, a glint in his eye, a smile on his face, and energy in everything he said. From his endless supply of jokes to his impassioned demand that Russian president Mikhail Gorbachev take down the Berlin wall, Reagan's communication skills were legendary. Some pundits christened him the "Teflon president" because no scandals or problems ever stuck to him. The American public was always ready to forgive him in response to his sincere apology and acceptance of responsibility. Neither Jimmy Carter nor Walter Mondale had a chance against such a likable, energetic communicator.

George Bush faced an opponent who, by all accounts, was a sensitive and brilliant man. Governor Michael Dukakis was intelligent, but his low-key and measured demeanor came across with all the excitement of reading the list of Smiths in the phone book. Nothing in his campaign communicated vision, energy, or passion. One of few memorable moments of his race for the White House came during a debate when journalist Bernard Shaw asked him about capital punishment and what his response would be if his wife were raped and murdered. When his answer lacked any passion at all, he came across as unfeeling and almost inhuman. Bush won a lopsided victory.

Four years later, however, Bush found himself in a different ball game. The election of 1992 pitted him against Governor Bill Clinton, a new style of communicator. Failing to grasp and communicate the "vision thing," Bush's popularity plummeted from the highest rating any president had ever enjoyed to an embarrassing defeat at the polls.

One of the starkest examples of what the lack of communication skill costs can be easily seen in the vice-presidential debates of 1992. Dan Quayle represented the Republican ticket, Al Gore the Democratic ticket, and standing for the upstart Reform Party of Ross Perot was Admiral James Stockdale. The Admiral was one of the finest Americans to ever run for office. A former war hero and long-term POW, Stockdale had become a brilliant Greek scholar after his return to civilian life and embarked on a new career. His brilliance was completely eclipsed, however, by his inability to communicate. Within thirty seconds of his opening statement, he experienced a total meltdown. He went blank and reached for his notes. He grabbed his glasses and put them on the end of his nose. He tried to get a line out three or four times. People watching the national broadcast felt as if they were watching him get hit by a two-ton truck. They sympathized, but they did not want this man one heartbeat from the presidency.

> In my library are about a thousand volumes of biography—a rough calculation indicates that more of these deal with men who have talked themselves upward than with all the scientists, writers, saints and doers combined. Talkers have always ruled. They will continue to rule. The smart thing is to join them.
> BRUCE BARTON (1886–1967)
> Scholar, editor, author, congressman, and founder of the ad agency Batten, Barton, Durstine, and Osborne

Apart from his politics and regardless of one's personal opinion either of the man or of his policies, Bill Clinton's ability as a communicator not only got him elected, but also helped the public overlook his admitted moral shortcomings. His ability to connect with an audience helped him overcome obstacles that would have been insurmountable for almost anyone else in the political world. Though he had no military service, he defeated bona fide war heroes Bush and Dole. Over and over the American public granted him pardon and latitude. Like Reagan, Clinton was often able to overwhelm even those diametrically opposed to his policies with his ability to communicate and connect with people. And at the end of his term of office, he had one of the highest favorability ratings of any president in history.

Our point is not to commend or criticize any of these politicians or their policies. We desire only to show you that history leads us to the inescapable conclusion that communicators are able to get people to see things their way. They get people to like and accept *them,* and then they have a platform for their *message.* Failure to communicate cannot be redeemed by brilliance, intelligence, sincerity, or even truth. No matter how great one's message, it cannot change those it does not reach. If politicians, who work for temporal gains and goals, understand and apply these principles, how much more should we who work for eternal results?

DIVINE POWER AND HUMAN MEANS

In some ways there is a tension between our dependence on the inherent power of the Word and our need to communicate well. We dare not think that our skill and ability can save anyone or make them grow in grace. We must constantly check ourselves lest we lapse from a commitment to excellence into claiming a share of God's glory. But by the same token, if we excuse our own laziness and do not use every tool at our disposal, we presume on God. We might as well not study, improve our education, learn vocabulary, or concern ourselves with our appearance. Remember, the better we are at communicating, the less others even notice *us* and the more they see *him*.

If we really understand the incredible power inherent in the gospel and if we have experienced the power of the Resurrection ourselves, how can we be unmoved and dispassionate about it?

J. Sidlow Baxter, a Christian writer and pastor, told the story of a lady named Beatrice Cleland, who had been won to Christ by the man who later served as her pastor. Reflecting on how God had used this man to help her find Jesus, she wrote a poem that encapsulates the way God uses human means for divine purposes.

Not only by the words you say
Not only by your deeds confessed
But in the most unconscious way
Is Christ expressed.
Was it a beatific smile
Or holy light upon your brow?
Oh, no. I felt His presence
When you laughed just now.
For me 'twas not the truth you taught
To you so clear, to me so dim,
But when you came to me
You brought a sense of Him.
And from your eyes He beckons me.
And from your lips His love is shed
Till I lose sight of you
And see the Christ instead.

Energy, passion, conviction—these are the essential ingredients of Christian communication. Enthusiasm and passion are not optional equipment but are critically important because the treasure of truth we handle is worth it. No other message in the world so deserves excitement and intensity.

The Affect-Meter

Affect is a term used by psychologists to describe the "feelings" side of our human makeup—our emotions, moods, and temperament. The affect-meter is a visual representation of physical and emotional energy and enthusiasm. To have "0 percent affect" is to have no emotional energy, to be completely unexpressive, flat, monotonous, colorless, and lifeless. To have "100 percent affect" is to be totally buoyant, exuberant, animated, and excited. The affect-meter swings according to how much energy we feel free to express. For some of us, unfortunately, the pointer has gotten stuck somewhere during our emotional development.

From birth to two years old, a human being is at full affect (maximum emotional energy). A young child expresses himself with virtually no inhibition at all.

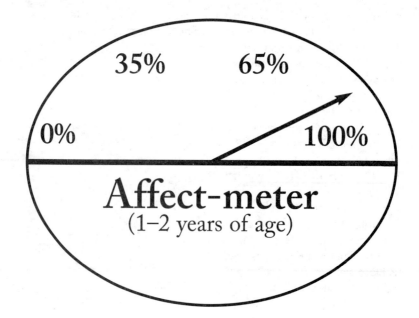

During the years from two to twelve, the momentum begins swinging to the left, toward narrow affect (minimum emotional energy). The natural exuberance of the child is gradually suppressed and deadened during the socialization process, which has both positive and negative results. In most people, this process gets out of balance, the meter swinging way over toward low energy/affect. The result is repression and inhibition.

During the teenage years, thirteen to nineteen, even though actual stifling has usually stopped, the meter remains down at narrow affect, resulting in the phase we call "the unexpressed years." This is the last habit pattern the child experiences, and the unrelenting forces of adolescent peer pressure reinforce this habit with a vengeance. Few teenagers escape the emotional pitfalls of the unexpressed years, and the adolescent patterns of awkwardness and shyness usually harden into inhibited adulthood.

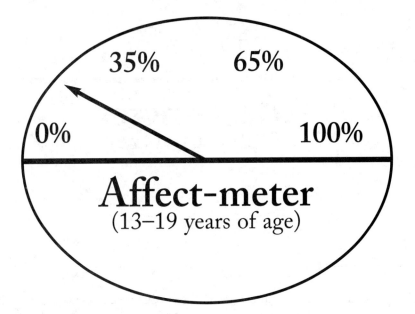

It is the exceptional young adult who has both the strong self-image and natural energy to break through this shell of repression on his own, and our inhibiting habit patterns continue to form and harden during the years from age twenty to thirty.

It's easy to see how we got the way we are. From our earliest years on into our twenties, thirties, and beyond we have been subject to forces and pressures to conform, to fit in, to be correct. These are all inhibiting forces, pushing us deep into the pit of minimal emotional energy.

But we don't have to remain there. We can learn to push the meter back to where it belongs—indeed, where it has always belonged.

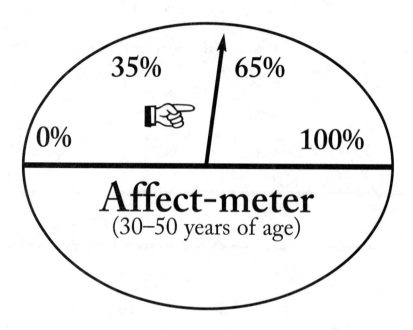

FULLY EXPRESSIVE COMMUNICATION

The most effective communicators are those who are expressive, yet fully in control. They are alive with energy, but they know boundaries. They consciously control the affect-meter in their own behavior. Very few of us have that kind of control. Instead, we are driven by unconscious habits laid down when we were children.

To become effective, we must relearn how to be fully expressive. We must rediscover the uninhibited state of the two-year-old, yet govern that expressiveness with the conscious control of a mature adult. We must consciously choose for the sake of our message to push that meter back to where it belongs.

The "Forward Lean" of Life

One of the simplest and easiest ways to communicate energetically and in a way that exudes confidence is to stand in what is called the "ready position." That simply means stand with your weight forward, your knees ever so slightly flexed so that you could bounce on the balls of your feet. You feel like an athlete ready to move quickly and easily in any direction. With your weight forward like this it is impossible to slouch on one hip or to rock back on your heels.

This position is one of those subconscious triggers that tell your listener that you are excited and interested in what you are saying. The lack of energy and a posture that leans away signals just the opposite—apathy and disinterest. When you are speaking confidently from a self-assured stance and attitude, your energy is directed forward, both physically and psychologically, toward your listener.

The reason we are introducing you to this small but important bit of information here is that we want this position to serve as a metaphor for your global attitude toward communication. Like the child who has great "affect," you are not inhibited but excited. Your whole attitude toward sharing the message God has given you is a forward lean! You are ready to flow rather than freeze. You are excited rather than nervous, enthusiastic rather than reluctant. Everything about you must convey that, above all else, you believe in God's message and in your message. You are completely committed to the truth that you share, whether it is sharing the gospel with a neighbor, teaching a lesson to your class, or telling your fourteen-year-old that you love her.

Sameness Is the Enemy

So for the Christian communicator, sameness is the enemy. If our message becomes mundane or has a routine tone, the natural mind can easily ignore it. In essence, the ears may hear it, but it never goes any deeper. Some preachers preach loud all the time, even to the point of screaming, but it still has little impact because that is *all* they do. Others are monotone, while yet others are very predictable—they *always* get loud at the same moments. Parishioners subconsciously learn to shut them out, just like the person who lives next to a railroad track never notices the train.

Preachers are not the only ones with this problem. Many Christians feel a burden to share their faith, so they dutifully memorize a canned presentation. But relying on rote memory has made them sound unenthusiastic and uninterested. The result is that there are no waves of energy to carry the message. The feeling brain senses a conflicting signal and gives greater weight to the visual and vocal than to the verbal. When you get one of those telemarketing calls on the phone, can't you tell the person is reading a message or has memorized it? Do you ever really listen to the canned safety speeches that the flight attendants give on an airplane? The monotonous way they do it begs you to do something else! Physical movement and energy are important for the same reason. We always find listening to a speaker who moves much easier than giving our attention to someone who just stands there. The brain is designed to notice movement as opposed to stillness.

Imagine that you are looking at a room full of furniture. No people or animals are in the room, only furniture, drapes, carpet, and wall hangings. The only sound you hear is the ticking of a grandfather clock that stands erect against the wall. You watch the room for several minutes, then your eye catches movement in one corner. A drape flutters in the wind, making only a slight noise, but the interruption in the visual field and in the slight noise from the same area draw your attention like a magnet. Your mind is drawn to the energy, the break in the sameness.

To speak with bold assurance, you have to exhibit energy so compelling that it will draw and hold the interest of your hearers. You need to speak with a passion that fits and highlights the great message God has given you, so that you get your information past the feeling brain and your listeners really see and hear what you have to say.

Part IV
The Nine Behavioral Skills

Effective communication is a wonderful balance between delivery and content, style and substance. Great communicators pay close attention to both elements. In addition, Christian communicators have the potential to become the greatest communicators in the world. If our message is biblical or based on scriptural principles, then it is unquestionably true and has the inherent power of the Holy Spirit that transcends any human message or capacity. In addition, the confidence that comes from knowing we can do all things through Christ who strengthens us and our deep conviction of the truth of the Word of God give us the bold assurance that is essential to connect with our hearers.

Such certainty should urge us into the forward lean that convinces our listeners of our excitement, passion, and conviction. We become a tool in God's hands that he uses to influence and persuade others that they need the assurance that we exhibit.

A Word Worthy of Work

It would be a great sin to present God's message in an unworthy manner. Realizing that God gave us the tools of communication so that we might best relay his message to others keeps us willing to work so that we might give God's Word the presentation that befits its divine origin. An ambassador must convey not only the content of his leader, but the character and temperament of the one who sent him.

To have the content and substance that gives our words power, we must saturate ourselves with the Word of God. We systematically and painstakingly study the Scriptures to learn life-giving and life-changing truth.

Improving our delivery and style so that we can best convey God's truth requires no less commitment. All communicators can learn how to develop the nine communication skills that make them most effective.

The Nine Communication Skills

Do you remember the nine skills that serve as the communicator's tools? These nine skills are the basis of good delivery and style that serve as the conduit for our message to reach the listener:

- *Eye communication:* the ability to make and maintain eye contact in a meaningful way.
- *Gestures and facial expression:* animation communicated through your face and body that corresponds with your message and conveys energy.
- *Posture and movement:* reflecting confidence and energy in your body position and movement.
- *Dress and appearance:* presenting yourself in a way that does not detract from the message you want your hearer to grasp.
- *Voice and vocal variety:* employing pitch, volume, and vocal energy that will keep your listener engaged in the content of what you are saying.
- *Words and fillers:* using language that is replete with meaning, effective pauses, and devoid of "fillers"—those annoying "ums," "ahs," and meaningless phrases such as "whatever," "you know," "like," and "I mean."
- *Humor:* a healthy sense of humor about yourself and life in general that makes you approachable and likable.
- *Listener involvement:* simple ways to involve yourself with your listeners— whether one or one thousand—in order to help them listen.
- *The "natural self":* using these communication parameters to let the real you come through without seeming stiff or phony.

If you want to develop your speaking ability, you must work on practicing these skills. In the following section you will learn each one more fully as well as some practical exercises that will help you implement them.

These exercises are simple but powerful. Beware of two responses that you might feel. First, "I already know that. I don't need to work on that." These exercises are designed to change what you do, not what you know. Even if you *know* them, you won't do them unless you consciously make yourself practice until you get to the place where you do them naturally and unconsciously.

The second response is "This feels silly. I don't think this will do anything." Almost anything feels silly the first time. Trust us, there is a disparity between how you feel and how you look! What really feels silly is when you have the opportunity to speak but you do it poorly because you have not learned these communication skills. The benefits you will experience almost immediately are worth any temporary discomfort you may feel.

These exercises are a new behavioral vocabulary for effective communicators. They develop a sensitivity and a control over your behavior as you learn how to open your listeners' feeling brain so your content can get in. They may seem simple, even common sense, but if they are not executed you will never be as effective as you could be.

CHAPTER II
Skill One: Eye Communication

Objective: to look at another person
steadily and confidently

The primary skill for gaining credibility is the ability to make and maintain eye contact. It has the greatest impact in both one-on-one communication and large-group communication. Your eyes literally connect your mind to someone else's since your eyes are the only part of your central nervous system that are in direct contact with another human being. When your eyes meet the eyes of another person, you make a feeling-brain-to-feeling-brain connection. When you fail to make that connection, it matters little what you say.

Many people are not even aware that they do not use their eyes effectively. There are several common problems that we need to overcome or avoid.

WHAT OTHERS DO

Eye-dart

Rhoda Bantry is a wonderful Christian mother who would like to have a greater impact in her church. But even in casual conversation after worship services, her eyes flit about like a child's looking around a toy store. If she keeps them still at all she usually looks at the person's shoulder rather than into their eyes. It gives others the feeling that she is hiding something.

The minister of education won't ask her to teach a class because he knows how people feel when they speak with her. She fails to connect with the feeling brain, and people find her eye-dart distracting and annoying. Predictably, she has little impact even though she has great insight into the Scriptures.

Greener grass gaze

John Loudon is a typical Type A personality. Full of energy and zest, he usually makes people feel unimportant and as though they are wasting his time.

When he is talking to someone at a convention or in the hallway at work, he is always looking around at who is walking by, searching for people he has to connect with, and occasionally waving to a passing acquaintance while conversing with someone else. He gives the obligatory nod to the person he is talking to, but they see him looking elsewhere and they feel as if he would rather be with someone else.

> An eye can threaten like a loaded and leveled gun; or can insult like hissing and kicking; or in its altered mood by beams of kindness, make the heart dance with joy.
> RALPH WALDO EMERSON

Prayer eyes

Jerry Walker is a young pastor in a small church who has to do everything, including leading worship. Sometimes, when he is singing, he closes his eyes and tilts his head back as though looking upward. But often when he is preaching he will go into that same closed-eye mode. He will keep his eyes closed for as long as five seconds at a time between glances at the congregation.

This habit carries over into his personal conversations, too, and his parishioners tend to view him as cold and detached—the exact opposite of the way Jerry sees himself and certainly not the way he wants to be perceived. Could it be that some of the tensions he feels around the church are not caused so much by any doctrinal differences, but by his undiagnosed "slo-blink?"

WHAT YOU CAN DO

Do you see yourself in one or more of these examples? If so, there's hope! These eye communication problems are curable. Don't assume that just making eye contact is enough. Eye contact implies a short glance will connect, but good eye communication means really looking at an individual—making a feeling-brain-to-feeling-brain connection.

Jesus undoubtedly saw people as individuals. Frequently the Gospels tell how he was moved with compassion as he looked at a crowd. People did not remain an impersonal mass of humanity to him, but individuals with specific needs who felt love and acceptance in his eyes.

The three I's of eye communication

Good eye communication is enhanced and fortified by remembering a few basic tips. First, *use involvement rather than intimidation or intimacy.* When you look at a person for a long time, you are either staring down or gazing longingly. To look at someone for twenty or thirty uninterrupted seconds would make most listeners feel uncomfortable. But, quite frankly, few speakers struggle with looking at listeners too long. Most exhibit the opposite tendency, even though most of our communication calls for involvement.

Look for five seconds

How then can you achieve that appropriate level of eye communication? How can you be certain that you have looked at audience members enough, but not too much? The answer is to count to five. A feeling of involvement requires about five seconds of steady eye contact, the time we normally take to complete a thought or a sentence. When we talk to another person and are excited, enthusiastic, and confident, we communicate best by looking at them for five to ten seconds. This is one way that a speaker before a large audience can still make each of them feel that they are individually important.

One warning is in order, however. If you are not accustomed to good eye communication, it will feel weird the first time you do it. Five seconds seems like an eternity. But the results are worth the temporary discomfort, so push beyond your comfort zone for longer eye communication. You'll get used to the change of habit.

Beware of eye-dart and slo-blink

When we lack confidence or feel the pressure, our instinct is to avoid the eyes of our listener and allow our eyes to dart around. We think we can hide our nervousness or lack of confidence, but the opposite is true. The listener can read our anxiety, and it subconsciously undermines our message. Like a scared rabbit, we exude the "aroma" of fear.

Whenever a person closes his or her eyes for two or three seconds, the listener intuits that the message is unexciting and unimportant. Slo-blink communicates "I don't really want to be here. Even I am bored with what I am saying." Listeners don't require a lot of time to determine that they feel the same way.

Get on video

For all of these eye communication deficiencies, as well as for many other problems you will encounter, one exercise stands head and shoulders above the rest. The quickest and most effective cure can be found in video feedback. Make a videotape of yourself speaking and then watch it carefully, focusing especially on your eye movements. Notice your length of contact and idiosyncrasies like eye-dart or slo-blink. Before watching yourself on tape you may be unaware of your habits and movements, but the tape will not lie!

Practice, practice, practice

Another helpful exercise is to practice one-on-one at every opportunity. Ask a faithful friend to notice your eye movements during a normal conversation. Have them count the number of times you blink, shift your gaze, look away, or make eye contact. Get an average count of how long you tend to look at a person and work at increasing your time until you can look at an individual for at least five seconds or more.

Even when you are alone, practice with a paper audience. By sticking Post-it notes with little happy faces on them around the room, you can get accustomed to looking at audience members for five seconds or more. Stick the notes on chairs, on the wall, or just around the room. Be certain that you put a face at the far fringes of the room, next to the corners so you learn to include the whole audience. As you make your presentation to your paper audience, focus on each individual, but work the whole room, corner to corner. As outlined below, you can also practice your movement with this exercise.

Even when you watch television you can increase your awareness and eye savvy by noticing real people in pressure situations. Observe people being interviewed, conversing with someone on a talk show, or making extemporaneous political commentary. Watch news shows in which interviewers put the heat on and get their subjects on the defensive. Notice how you feel about the person based on his response. Do you notice more what he says, or *how* he says it? The feeling brain reveals itself primarily through eye communication. You can notice the unmistakable signs of fear, anger, confidence, credibility, or disbelief. Sensitize yourself to the importance of eye communication and how it enhances or betrays a speaker's credibility and general likeability.

As you employ these exercises and eye communication becomes habitual, you will notice that you feel less nervous and you appear confident. Remember that it is not a problem for you to *feel* nervous, only to *appear* nervous. As you gain experience, you learn how to convert that nervousness into a positive energy that propels you forward. This breeds confidence, focuses your thoughts, and motivates your audience. You convey the power of your message through your eyes more than through any other single avenue of communication, so it is worth all the effort and practice.

CHAPTER 12

Skill Two: Gestures and Facial Expressions

Objective: to be relaxed and natural— open and energetic

The feeling brain is always sizing up whether or not a speaker really believes his message, and one of the primary measurements it uses is the level of animation. To communicate successfully, you must be enthused, excited, and speak with conviction and passion. Your listener's feeling brain is automatically and immediately determining how you *feel* about what you are saying.

An open-armed gesture and a warm, open smile are welcoming. It invites the listener in as your smile dominates your listener's impression of you and of your message. A smile shows on your mouth and around your eyes. It demonstrates openness, amiability, and credibility. The feeling brain naturally closes the shutters on a closed body and a face that is not smiling. It may even perceive the messenger as a threat.

The visual component of spoken communication is the most critical, and it is decided largely by your level of gesture and facial expression. These reveal our inner state and when active and open propel our message with energy and emotional force.

WHAT OTHERS DO

Convicting passion

Think of Billy Graham as he preaches. Hundreds of thousands of people who are otherwise hostile to the gospel still watch him on television or attend his crusades because they see in him conviction and passion. Even if they do not believe his message, many listen because they know *he* believes it. His open gestures and his gentle and fatherly smile are convincing evidence that his message is genuine. No one—kings, presidents, or peasants—feels threatened by Billy Graham, even if they reject his message. Dr. Graham makes certain that his manner never gets in the way of his message.

Wooden gestures

In the presidential election of 2000, one of the most-discussed aspects of the campaign was Al Gore's "stiff" appearance. He came across as wooden, unfeeling, and distant, often seeming to lecture his listeners. It may have been the critical factor that kept an incumbent party in a robust economy from running away with the election.

The fig-leaf flasher

Dennis Jefferson participated in a videotape seminar in which he gave a two-minute introduction. He started with a nervous gesture called the "fig leaf," the bad habit of clasping hands together and holding them just below the waistline. But he quickly switched into something much worse. He began raising his cupped hands every two seconds. When he saw it later on video playback, he called himself the "fig-leaf flasher." He was so shocked at the distraction that he immediately worked to change his habit and never "flashed" again.

> *We don't "know" our presidents. We imagine them. We watch them intermittently and from afar, inferring from only a relatively few gestures and reactions what kind of people they are and whether they should be in charge. Much depends on our intuition and their ability at a handful of opportune moments to project qualities we admire and respect.*
> MEG GREENFIELD

WHAT YOU CAN DO

Find your nervous gesture

Video feedback may reveal that you suffer from one or more common gesture problems. One of the most distracting ones is the fig-leaf gesture, mentioned above, but there are a catalog of nervous gestures that you can visualize, like "parade rest," "the arm lock," "the pocket-change jangler," "the hand washer," etc. Obviously one's message can easily get lost in the distraction that any nervous gesture causes. Find out what your nervous gesture is (we each have one) and do anything but that one.

Hands at your sides when not in use

Often we feel awkward when we let our hands rest at our sides, but this position looks composed and centered as a rest position. Watch to see how few people actually do that and how effective it can be as a base for gesturing.

Remember that there is a principle of disparity at work. If you are basically introverted and unaccustomed to using gestures, the slightest hand movement may feel like you are making windmills with your arms. If you watch yourself on video, however, you will see that your movement is not exaggerated at all.

> *A little sleep, a little slumber, a little folding of the hands to rest— and poverty will come on you like a bandit and scarcity like an armed man.*
> PROVERBS 6:10–11

Express yourself

Escape the poverty caused by communication gridlock and express yourself freely in both gestures and facial expression.

Practice by exaggerating. Exaggerate your gestures and your facial expressions. Video yourself and see if you can go over the top. Can you gesture too much? Smile too much? Try it, then watch the video. You'll see that you cannot overexaggerate. Not only will you learn that your gestures and smiles look good and are effective, but you will defuse your inhibitions and become less fearful. If you practice in situations when you can experiment and in which you feel no pressure, you will automatically be bigger without thinking about it when you are in a more critical situation.

One of the greatest methods of practice is to imitate an "expressor," someone who is an expressive role model. It doesn't have to be someone you like, just someone you can have fun imitating in an uninhibited way. Try to get inside that person's skin. Watch a video of an expressive preacher like Adrian Rogers, and then pretend that you are him. Imitate his movement, his gestures, his expressive face. Maybe mimicking some secular comedian like Phyllis Diller, Robin Williams, or Mel Brooks would be a good exercise. Try to become that energetic, expressive person, and you will unharness your own hidden energy.

Smile to become feeling-brain friendly

A person with a natural unsmiling face may, upon first trying to smile, feel that he is exhibiting the most toothsome grin in history. Others, watching the same event, may think, "Why is he so grim?" In reality few people truly exaggerate their gestures or facial expressions, no matter how hard they try. Remember the fact of disparity. Just video yourself trying to overdo it and you will be stunned when you watch it. The gestures and expressions that seemed so over the top will look very natural and appropriate on video.

Another problem that undermines your message is neglecting to smile appropriately. You need not grin like a Cheshire cat to get your point across, but failing to smile when you are telling the good news is unforgivable. Parents undermine their relationship with their children, employers harm their employees, and pastors lose their congregations when they fail to smile. If you think of the people whose company you most enjoy, you will realize that most of them smile a lot.

> *An unfriendly man pursues selfish ends; he defies all sound judgment.*
> PROVERBS 18:1

Lift your apples

If you find that you have trouble smiling, think of the upper part of your cheeks as apples. Smiling is just "lifting your apples," but what a difference it makes in your communication.

Have you ever thought about why little children wanted to be around Jesus? Nothing attracts little children and makes them feel more secure than a smile. Very early they learn that smiling people comfort them, care for them, coddle them. People who don't smile tend to neglect them, scold them, even hurt them. For the rest of our lives we feel drawn to smiling people. It makes little sense to tell people that Jesus is the greatest man who ever lived, that he offers the greatest gift ever given, and that this is the best news they have ever heard and to do it without a smile. Lift those apples!

Your smile even affects you. It lifts your spirits. It generates more energy. You feel the smile throughout your whole body. But beware—phony smiles don't work. Quite frankly, they look phony. We aren't suggesting that you learn how to fake it. We are suggesting that you comprehend that your message is good news and that you let it give you a real smile.

You will find that good gestures and a smile will free you to share your thoughts fully. You will find a ready audience, because when you smile, the world smiles with you. Your gestures show openness that people find inviting. The gestures you use naturally emphasize your most important points and concepts as your movement highlights your content. A warm smile and kinetic gestures go a long way to demonstrating the bold assurance God has given you through his Word.

CHAPTER 13

Skill Three: Posture and Movement

Objective: to stand tall and move with an ease and confidence

Think of the best speakers you know. Preachers, politicians, or presidents may qualify. Are any of them "slumpers?" Can you imagine Ronald Reagan in Berlin, lazily slouching as he demanded, "Mr. Gorbachev, tear down this wall!" There aren't many slumpers to be found among elite communicators, and for good reason. Confidence is expressed through good, upright posture. Your physical position reflects your mental readiness, and it is a decisive factor in how others see you and judge the credibility of your message.

In the first few seconds after people meet someone, they make assumptions about the speaker's level of confidence, competence, and credibility. Poor posture seriously undermines the trust and openness of our listeners.

Tall people often hunch over because they grew fast or early and perhaps felt self-conscious. Height, however, was not the problem—self-consciousness was. Still others slump because of a related weakness—they stick their nose in a manuscript or notes, so they slouch over to read them.

WHAT OTHERS DO

The power of posture

In Og Mandino's book *The Choice,* the character Ledesaibes says, "Some men are born to wear a tuxedo, and David Coronet is one of them. Standing ramrod straight at the single microphone of the ballroom's low stage, he looked like the chairman of the board of the entire world. He waited calmly, hands clasped in front of him, until the room quieted down."

The power of movement

Few pastors in America have had a greater impact on younger preachers than Adrian Rogers, pastor of the Bellevue Baptist Church in Memphis, Tennessee. From the moment he strides onto the platform until his exit after the last amen, Dr. Rogers's posture and movement communicate a readiness and attunement to the worship service that sets the tone for everyone in the seven-thousand-seat sanctuary.

> *Stand tall. The difference between towering and cowering is totally a matter of inner posture. It's got nothing to do with height, it costs nothing and it's more fun.*
> MALCOLM FORBES

During the musical worship, Dr. Rogers sits directly facing the audience with back straight, tall and erect, with both feet planted on the floor, looking as though he is ready to spring into action at any moment. When it's time for him to welcome guests, the pastor moves with excitement, confidence, and purpose. While preaching, Dr. Rogers also moves resolutely about the platform. No one doubts that he *owns* that space.

Credibility slouches

Author and commentator William F. Buckley is one of America's brightest and most colorful personalities, but he is better read than watched. Often on television to expound his views, he slouches in his chair as though he can barely stay awake, occasionally widening his narrow eyes, stuttering through broken sentences, and rarely changing his tone. He has such a keen mind and wit—think how powerful he could be if his posture just matched the alertness of his intellect.

Acting the part

Jim was a bright seminarian, but he was terrified to stand in front of a crowd and teach a lesson or preach. He had finally resigned himself to becoming a military chaplain because he thought that would require little public speaking. The first time he preached in a seminary classroom, he was frightened, and his posture showed it. With coaching and feedback he learned to stand erect, to move confidently about the platform, and to use a forward lean. The more adept he became at looking confident, the more confident he actually became.

By the end of the semester, Jim was an assured and accomplished speaker. Within a few months he became the pastor of a church where he had a great impact and grew to love the very thing that had once intimidated him.

What You Can Do

The posture basics

Whatever your reasons for slouching, some basic rules will help you stand with confidence and credibility. First, stand tall. Posture and poise go together, so stand with your shoulders back and your stomach in. Stand straight and move naturally, knees slightly bent rather than locked and rigid.

Watch your lower body. You may limit your effectiveness and negate your energy if you rock back on one hip. That communicates that you really don't want to be there and distances you from your listener, even in casual conversations. Common variations of this mistake are rocking from side to side or going forward and back from heel to toe.

Forward lean in thought and deed

Think of the concept of forward lean as not only something to do, but a way to be. That means that you always are in a state of readiness—leaning forward to volunteer, to do, to say. Physically you will lean slightly forward, knees somewhat flexed. Keep your weight on the balls of your feet. Like an athlete in the ready position, you are ready and able to move easily and quickly in any direction.

Communication rides on energy, and your posture indicates either interest and energy and a forward lean, or else it communicates apathy and disinterest and a laying back. Direct your energy forward, physically and psychologically, toward your listener. In this position you are always ready to communicate in any situation, formal or informal.

Move

No matter how strong the temptation to stay in one place, whether behind a pulpit or a lectern, resist that temptation! Get out and move and you will make emotional contact with your listeners. You will convey excitement, enthusiasm, and confidence in your movement. Remove any physical obstacle between you and your audience, such as the traditional lectern or podium. They are great note holders, but also great energy blockers. Move to the side.

Be careful of pacing back and forth, but move in a natural and purposeful way. Let your eye communication motivate your movement so that you move toward the person you are looking at. Take at least two steps at a time rather than a single tentative step. If you normally stand behind a lectern, come out from behind it and push yourself to get at least two steps away. That forces you to direct your energy forward and to learn to remove the barriers between you and your audience.

An easy exercise

You can practice both posture and movement by standing straight against a wall, your heels, buttocks, and head all touching the wall. Now walk away from the wall, being careful to hold that erect posture. You may feel stiff, but rest assured that you look great. If you want to video yourself to see the disparity in how it feels and how it looks, then go ahead. You will be convinced. You *can* improve your posture.

Like the eye exercise, you can also practice with a paper audience. With Post-it notes stuck around the room, give your presentation and let your eye communication motivate your movement. Move to one side of the room, plant your feet in the ready position, make good eye communication with your paper audience, then move directly and purposefully to the other side and do the same thing there.

As always, use video feedback to watch posture and movement. While other people can give you feedback and share their opinions, they are subjective and may not notice some things. The video captures all and is objective. And as you push yourself to stand erect, focus forward on your audience, and move out and connect with them, you will see that it looks great on video. You appear natural, relaxed, and confident. Bold assurance becomes the hallmark of your presentation because you feel taller, you look more confident, and your movement energizes both you and your audience.

CHAPTER 14

Skill Four: Dress and Appearance

Objective: to be appropriate to your environment in dress and grooming

After posture, the most immediate visual impression you make on your listener's feeling brain is dress and appearance. The impressions made in the first three seconds are so vivid that it takes another three minutes to add 50 percent more impression—whether negative or positive. Since those first three seconds are almost entirely visual, appearance determines the immediate receptivity of your audience. So if you make a poor first impression, even before you open your mouth, it takes a long time and a lot of work to overcome it.

Dress and appearance communicate who we are—our values, self-image, and self-respect. Whether you sport a pin-striped suit or a green mohawk, you choose a look to communicate something about yourself. You're sending a message. Your goal is not to impress your audience, but to make listeners feel comfortable and identify with you. Dress should not only be appropriate to who you are, but it should also be consistent with your message as well.

WHAT OTHERS DO

Right coat in the right place

Ever since Joseph wore his coat of many colors, clothes and appearance have communicated a message. More than that, our appearance affects the way we feel about ourselves.

Shawn Miller prided himself on his casual approach to ministry. He was convinced that he was going to be approachable, casual, and comfortable in the ministry, so he preached in jeans and flannel shirts, and he let his hair grow long. If Shawn had been pastoring in lumberjack country, his strategy may have worked.

Unfortunately, his church was in a suburban, upscale community. Church members were so embarrassed by his appearance that they felt uncomfortable inviting others to church, even though his preaching was otherwise biblical and engaging. His dress was too great an obstacle, however, and soon he found himself faced with losing half his church or his job.

Appropriate to the setting

In past years great preachers like W. A. Criswell of First Baptist Church in Dallas, Texas, or R. G. Lee of Bellevue Baptist in Memphis were identified by their bright white suits and fresh boutonnieres. Today pastors like Rick Warren of Saddleback Valley Community Church in southern California or Bill Hybels of Willow Creek in Chicago can get away with golf shirts, no ties, and even Hawaiian shirts (in Warren's case). Corporate America has established casual dress as the norm on Fridays. Neither a white suit nor a Hawaiian shirt can fit all situations. What makes these speakers successful is that they dressed *appropriately* for their own cultural context.

> *You never get a second chance to make a good first impression.*
> JOHN MOLLOY

The former first lady's look

No one has demonstrated the effect of personal appearance more than former First Lady Hillary Rodham Clinton. Her advisers continued to experiment with hairstyles and clothing throughout the Clintons' years in the White House. To their credit, they largely succeeded.

Early in the Clinton years, the first lady had a very high negative rating and was disliked by many Americans. Her thick glasses, hair tucked beneath a hairband, and dowdy style of dress were simply not flattering.

After getting advice from makeup artists and hairstylists, Mrs. Clinton's image changed drastically. Glasses were replaced by contacts, her hairstyle was updated, and unfashionable clothing gave way to smart business suits. Her favorable ratings with the public rose for many reasons, but a sizeable part of that was congruity in dress and appearance with the status of first lady.

WHAT YOU CAN DO

Be appropriate for your audience

Dress, fashion, and style vary according to place and time, so there are no hard and fast rules about *what* to wear, but a few basic guidelines will help you keep your message central and avoid mistakes that undermine its impact.

First and foremost, be appropriate. Such a rule presupposes that you know your audience. If you are speaking somewhere for the first time, be sure you investigate enough to determine what dress is appropriate. Most businesses and churches, for instance, develop their own corporate culture, which includes a certain mode of dress. Even as corporate America has adopted a more casual dress code, so have many churches. Some churches and companies staunchly maintain a traditional Sunday-best fashion requirement. Keep in mind that fitting in is worth it.

The best speakers always get themselves out of the way. In the very same way that nervous habits distract a listener from the message, so sloppy dress or flashy fashion can force the wrong focus. An appropriate style of clothing that fits in with the surrounding culture is always best because it does not draw attention to the wrong thing.

Be appropriate to yourself

Be certain that your dress makes you feel comfortable and at ease with yourself. If you wear a tie, for instance, don't wear a shirt whose collar is too tight and tempts you to tug at it while you speak (not to mention that a tight collar is terrible for your vocal chords). Bear in mind the norms of the group, the social setting, the time of day, and the weather.

Some D&A tips

- Conservative dress is usually better for a spiritual message.
- Dress and groom up, not down. Better to overdress than to underdress if you are unable to know the norms ahead of time.
- For women, if you are in doubt about whether to wear slacks, don't. A skirt or a dress is almost always acceptable, but pants may make a statement that you don't want to make.
- Dress and groom at the conscious level rather than just according to habit. Don't just dress the same way you always have or wear the same colors. Ask if your mode of dress is effective. Make choices at the conscious level, especially mindful of how it will appear to those you want to influence.
- Remember that the first appearance instantly communicates how you feel about yourself and even about your audience.

- Button your jacket when you are standing. Some women's jackets are tailored to be unbuttoned, but men's suits and jackets are tailored to be buttoned for a smart look. It communicates a sharp, neat, and organized feel. Make sure that the jacket is a proper fit.

Get people feedback

This is one area in which people feedback may be more important than video feedback because style is subjective. It pays to find out what *others* think about your appearance, and you do that by asking. Men need to ask about clothing, hair, beard and moustache (if they have one), and jewelry. Women should ask about clothing and accents, haircut and hairstyle, makeup, and jewelry. Seek honest appraisals from a variety of people.

Observe others

In addition to the personal feedback you get from others, you should also be extra observant. Read current magazines on style. If you hear a great speaker, pay attention to how his clothing affects your perception of him and your acceptance of the message. John Molloy's classic *Dress for Success* is a helpful, if opinionated, digest of extensive research on the subject. Above all, notice what others around you are wearing, but don't try to become a carbon copy of *anyone* else. Be yourself—the best and smartest *you* possible.

As a result, you will feel confident in how you look. Eventually you will take less time in dressing and grooming because you will know what you are doing and why. Most importantly, you will make a positive and lasting impression that will add to your overall effectiveness.

THE VISUAL IMPACT SKILLS

These first four of the nine communication skills have one thing in common: they transform our visual impact. These are the skills that listeners will notice immediately, visually, and will cause them to let our message past the feeling brain. The next four are energy skills, which help us pack more energy into our message and help our listeners become and stay involved with our message. As with the other skills, you will see how easy it is to put the energy factor into your communication and to experience the kind of impact you want when you speak.

CHAPTER 15
Skill Five: Voice and Vocal Variety

Objective: to use your voice as a
rich, resonant instrument

Your voice is a wonderfully expressive instrument, a tool with a range of ability with infinite possibility and precision. Few people stop to think about their voice, but great communicators pay special attention to this instrument.

Your voice is the vehicle that carries your message. While some people treat it like an old truck, you should realize that it is a Porsche. You can push it, open it up, and let it soar. The voice is the primary means of transmitting your energy and infusing your message with a sense of direction and importance.

The feeling brain is finely attuned to the voice. It hears nuance and seeks meaning in volume, pitch, and especially in tone. A single word can reveal volumes of information about you. If you are skeptical, just make a phone call to someone you know well. Listen as she says hello. Often you can tell if she is rushed, aggravated, disturbed by the interruption, in a good mood, or excited. How many arguments have married couples waged over the tone or volume of a single word? Parents often recognize the attitude of their teens by noticing their tone or speech pattern.

The human voice has an infinite variety and capacity to communicate meaning that goes far beyond the bare dictionary meaning of the words. You are undoubtedly aware of this capacity when you listen to others, but have you ever listened to your own voice on tape? Were you pleased or embarrassed? Perhaps you said something like, "That doesn't sound like me!" In reality, the voice on the tape is truer to your "real" voice than the one you hear as you speak. The voice on tape is carried by sound waves through the air, but the voice you hear yourself also travels by vibration through bones in your head.

What Others Do

A memorable voice of the past

Martin Luther King's "I Have a Dream" speech, given from the steps of the Lincoln Memorial, was one of the greatest and most memorable speeches in American history. Dr. King's greatest tool was his voice. Every American who has heard that speech can still conjure up its clear echoes in memory. His lilting vibrato, the quickening pace of his words, the rise and fall of his pitch are forever recorded in the national consciousness. Can you imagine Dr. King's speech in a monotone?

> *The Devil hath not, in all his quiver's choice, an arrow for the heart like a sweet voice.*
> LORD BYRON

Monotony lulls to sleep

Robert is a well-known author. He has written two blockbuster, nonfiction best-sellers on new trends in business. Chris, a professional speaker, was fascinated with Robert's ideas, and drove two hundred miles to hear him speak. Chris fell asleep within fifteen minutes. Robert's flat, dull monotone became a barrier to the exciting vibrancy of his ideas.

A memorable voice in the present

During the impeachment trial of President Clinton, most Americans got their first glimpse of Lloyd John Ogilvie, chaplain of the United States Senate. Every day before the legal battle began, Dr. Ogilvie would stand beside the chief justice of the United States and lead a prayer. Though the proceedings themselves attracted controversy, Dr. Ogilvie's voice, perhaps the deepest *basso profundo* ever heard on American television, received unanimity in comment by the pundits and observers. When he speaks, his voice fills the Senate chamber like God thundering from Mount Sinai or speaking from heaven.

What You Can Do

Record yourself

To hear ourselves as others hear us, we have to record ourselves—whether on the phone, in casual conversation, in a meeting, or giving a formal speech. Though you may find listening to yourself a bit uncomfortable at first, it is worth it because a recording is the only way you can really know how much energy you transmit when you speak. And if you really *hear* your voice, you'll be able to *change* your voice.

Make your voice naturally authoritative

Not everyone is blessed with a deep, resonant, and authoritative voice like James Earl Jones or Adrian Rogers, but everyone can learn how to speak in a lower register. With just a few minutes of practice and a conscious effort to speak in a lower voice, you can begin to develop a voice that more effectively gets and keeps attention. (See the "King Kong" exercise on page 85.)

Use the full range of your voice

God has given us an incredible vocal range, yet most people use only about 30 percent of that range when they speak. Treat your voice like a roller coaster. Let it change its pace and its pitch. Let it rise and fall with the meaning of your words. Make it express emotion and emphasize your message with appropriate changes in pitch. Remember: "sameness" is the enemy! A monotone voice, no matter how great the content, will put others to sleep. So lift that voice over the summit, then let it plummet. As you picture the roller coaster when you speak, it develops your range and makes you aware of your full vocal toolbox.

Be aware of your telephone voice

Remember Dr. Albert Mehrabian whose research we cited in chapter 8? Not only did he discover that the vocal and visual account for 93 percent of a person's appraisal of credibility, but he also found something important about the voice. His research indicates that your voice—intonation, resonance, and auditory delivery—accounts for as much as 84 percent of your emotional impact and believability when people can't see you, such as on the phone or on an audiotape!

So the opinion a listener forms about the credibility or the level of importance of your message derives specifically from how you use your voice. Surprisingly, most people are less expressive and energetic on the phone than in person. Particularly in leaving voice-mail messages, people tend to get "information heavy" and talk in a monotone. Your goal should be to use the kind of passion and energy on the phone that you would use in face-to-face situations.

Put a smile in your voice

Smile as you talk! Can you hear a smile from a happy person on the phone? Well, they can hear whether you are smiling or not too. Practice "smiling" with a tape recorder. You will be amazed at the difference you hear. As you become conscious of the emotional signals your voice sends, you become conscious of the importance of letting your voice show happiness, excitement, and enthusiasm.

Do the "King Kong"

For a great exercise to relax your vocal chords before a big speech and to lower your voice generally, do the King Kong exercise. Here's how it goes:

Let your mouth drop open. Inhale deeply through your nose—a deep breath from the diaphragm. Now, exhale. And as you exhale, say or sing the words, "King Kong, ding dong, bing bong," in an up-and-down, sing-song fashion. Start at a medium pitch and lower the tone, word by word, toward the deepest range of your voice. Let the words drop in tone like stones falling down a hilly mountainside into the valley below. Make that last "bong" into a three-syllable word, and drop it in steps to the bottom of your range. Gently, now! Don't strain your throat muscles reaching for that basso profundo! Again, the goal is to relax your voice so that it can find a deeper register.

Repeat this several times. If you do this regularly (daily) you can permanently lower your voice. It's much like daily weightlifting—as long as you keep exercising you will get increased strength in your muscles. But stop exercising, and the muscle turns to flab.

Use voice mail

Many of us have access to voice-mail systems in our company. It is growing fast in the home market, too, so most will be able to use it now, or soon, in a new way—to practice communication skills. Use it as a feedback tool. Send yourself a copy of a real message you are sending to a colleague or friend, and listen to the sound of your voice. Do it daily at first, then weekly. Begin experimenting with some of these concepts and hear your voice take on new life and give new meaning to your words.

CHAPTER 16

Skill Six: Words and Fillers

Objective: to use words well, and use the power of the pause

To say that words are powerful and a great way to infuse our message may seem obvious. Yet a common way to undermine their power and suck the life out of our words is through the use of fillers, words and nonwords that have no real meaning.

Selecting the right words for the right situation and understanding and using the right nuance and connotations of words make the difference between giving a speech and being a communicator. A rich, varied vocabulary and the ability to use it appropriately make the difference between good enough and great!

Yet so many conversations, speeches, and sermons are filled with the ugly nonword fillers like "um," "and," "you know" and, in the teenage world, "like totally." Although "um" and "ah" are the most common, there are dozens of nonwords, but the debilitating fact is their monotonous repetition, their verbal redundancy. So choose your words, and pauses, well.

"A word fitly spoken," says Proverbs 25:11 (KJV), "is like apples of gold in pictures of silver."

WHAT OTHERS DO

Good examples

Listen to great speakers for noteworthy expressions and turns of phrase. Read *Reader's Digest* features like "Toward More Picturesque Speech." When you read a novel, notice not just *what* the author says, but *how* she says it. Listen to accomplished speakers in the corporate lecture circuit.

Words in print

Some of the most memorable sermons ever preached remain powerful, even years later and now only in print, because they employ powerful, picturesque words to represent God's message of truth. Jonathan Edwards's classic "Sinners in the Hands of an Angry God" still reverberates with incredible emotional power and effect after two hundred years. R. G. Lee's "Payday Someday" is another fine example of an excellent vocabulary used to maximum effect and yet never at the expense of comprehension and accessibility.

> *Perhaps of all the creations of man, language is the most astonishing.*
> LYTTON STRACHEY

Words that overcome

David Miller, a Southern Baptist evangelist from Arkansas, likes to call himself "just a country preacher," but his self-effacing title belies the tremendous reputation he has as a great communicator of God's Word.

In addition to the typical difficulties inherent in full-time evangelism, David has to contend with the additional problems associated with the crippling and mysterious disease of muscular atrophy. Suffering from this debilitating disease since he was fifteen, David is now confined to a wheelchair and unable to move and gesture when he preaches. Just as he has faced and conquered the physical challenges of everyday life, so he has learned to compensate for those communication skills he cannot use due to his handicap. Preaching from a wheelchair, David is unable to move on the platform or even to gesture with his hands. He cannot hold a Bible or look at notes. A gifted expositor of the Word, David understands that he still needs to infuse his message with energy and passion that will keep his audience involved with his message.

So how does he do it? He uses the most vivid facial expressions and picturesque language imaginable. He memorizes his biblical text and the outline of his sermon. His words are precise yet always comprehensible to his audience. He makes an emotional connection through words that carry the biblical content to the hearts and minds of his audience. If anyone doubts the power of language, he need look no further than a communicator like David Miller to see just how potent a rich vocabulary can be.

Watch the professionals

Nothing gets attention as easily and yet as effectively as a pause. It interrupts the barrage of sound and indicates a thoughtful deliberation. The pause indicates that what is to follow is momentous, worth listening to, and profound. If you watch videos of great comedians and communicators, not only will you notice that they pause frequently, but you can even notice that you can usually count three between setup and delivery, between question and answer, between joke and punch line. Bill Cosby, for instance, is a master of the pause, using it to let comedic expectation and laughter build while he makes a funny face or allows the humor to sink in.

What You Can Do

Build your vocabulary

The English language is a powerful tool, loaded with extra attachments and gadgets called synonyms. Because of the wealth of synonyms in our language, we can take a single thought and express it in hundreds of ways. With a well-stocked vocabulary at our disposal, we can speak with precision, with subtle shades of meaning, with evocative imagery, and most of all with energy.

That does not mean that we have to know and use a lot of "big words." We should have at our disposal the power to communicate in a variety of ways. We should have an entire warehouse of words immediately available. We should know how to say "meticulous" instead of "careful," "conundrum" instead of "riddle," "pivotal" instead of "crucial," "endow" instead of "give," "disciple" instead of "follower," "rebuff" instead of "refuse," and *"ad infinitum"* (or *even "ad nauseum"*) instead of "and so on and so forth," or worse yet, "yada yada yada."

With a little effort and intention, it's easy to stretch your vocabulary. Just try to use one new word a day. If you come across a new word while you're reading a book or a magazine, jot it down, look it up in a dictionary, start using it in conversation, and make it your own. Your purpose is not to show off, but to communicate effectively. A strong vocabulary is a powerful tool in your communication toolbox. Continually be on the lookout for new words that can help you communicate in the clearest, most colorful, most interesting way for every situation.

Paint word pictures

Language can do more for our message than give us multiple ways of expressing an idea. Language can pack the energy factor into our communication by enabling us to paint intense, colorful word pictures. We can lend the energy of both motion and emotion to our speech by the use of metaphors and vivid expressions.

With a little imaginative language, the night sky becomes a "sparkling cosmic ocean." An F-16 fighter-bomber becomes a "screaming bird of prey." A freeway at night becomes "a river of glowing red coals." The stock market doesn't just go down, it "plummets."

These are not "big words" used to impress other people with how smart we are. They are fairly simple words, but put together in ways that create memorable, exciting images that make vivid impressions on the feeling brain of our listener. Our goal is not to impress, but to make an impression. A rich and varied language can be one of the best tools at our command for getting our point across with energy and impact.

Beware of jargon

Have you ever talked to a doctor about your medical condition? Did you ask her to translate it for you? If she used medical jargon, you probably felt lost and ignorant, which is exactly how we make others feel when we use a specialized vocabulary they don't know.

Christianity has its own language, so be careful! Among insiders, jargon can be a convenient form of shorthand communication. Maybe other mature believers know what "washed in the blood of the lamb" or "concupiscence" or "propitiation" means, but does your audience? Make sure that your audience actually understands what you are saying. Technical terms that they don't understand slam their feeling brains shut.

———————————————————

Professor Calvin Miller, author of *The Singer* and many other popular books as well as a great teacher of preaching, understands the ease with which Christians lapse into church jargon and clichés that may be incomprehensible to the unchurched. In a parody he writes, "After all there have been many times when we've seen one set of footprints and knew we'd been touched by the Master's hand. And since then we've just been praisin' the Lord, cause we know that where we go hereafter depends on what we go after here. We ain't what we oughta' be, we ain't what we gonna' be, we ain't what we wanna' be, but thank God we ain't what we used to be, ever since we learned we had to either turn or burn. The key to our faith is that we had to stop trying and start trusting, 'cause in this life you gotta' either get right or get left. Since we got the joy of the Lord we've been shoutin', happy, and lookin' for the rapture. So we've found a hiding place, along with all those who've been saved, sealed, and delivered. But P.T.L.! I sure do talk the talk best when I walk the walk, wearing my W.W.J.D. bracelet. One day at a time, that's how I do it. After all, what you can't bless, you'd better confess. And I'm gonna' keep on keepin' on 'till we all gather at the river and I get the starch in my gown and the stars in my crown. 'Cause I know we're gonna' all meet again, here, there, or in the air."[1]

Find your level of fillers

Video yourself in conversation, teaching a class, or giving a speech. We can't overemphasize the power of feedback to uncover your communicating weaknesses so you can deal with them. As you listen or watch yourself on tape, count the fillers you use. You will probably wince a lot as you listen, but you'll also become more aware. That awareness will help you control the nonword habit.

Use the power of the pause

You're probably thinking, "But what if I can't live without my fillers? What happens if there's a big silent gap in my sentence while I'm thinking of the next phrase? Don't I need to fill those gaps with some sort of sound?" No! You fill those gaps with something infinitely more powerful than meaning-less sounds. You fill those gaps with something that gives energy and drama to your message: the pause. Did you know that the pause can be one of your most dynamic communication tools? You can pause for as long as three or four seconds—right in the middle of a sentence—and it will not only seem perfectly natural to your listener, it will give extra punch to your message.

> The notes I handle no better than many pianists. But the pauses between the notes . . . ah, that is where the art resides!
> ARTHUR SCHNABEL

The problem with pausing is that most of us have never tried it. We are afraid of silence in our communication. We're not used to pausing, so we rush to fill the silence with inane and meaningless sound—sound that dampens our energy factor and blunts the point of our message.

Some Basic Exercises. Exercises in pausing probably have the second biggest and most immediate payoff in your communication effectiveness.

(Eye communication is number one.) You will not only get rid of meaning-less fillers, but in gaining the power of the pause, you gain thinking time and can add drama to your impact.

Record yourself. Use video or audiotaping regularly to practice leaving pauses and to sensitize yourself to your patterns of fillers. It won't take long for you to sharpen your ear to those irritants. In fact, you'll soon begin catching yourself before the filler comes out of your mouth! You'll replace it with a pause. Being conscious of fillers is the first step to eliminating them.

Use voice mail. Use your voice-mail system as a feedback tool. Send your-self a copy of a real message you are sending to a colleague or friend, and listen to your pauses or fillers. Do it daily at first.

Practice with a buddy. Have a friend listen while you give an impromptu talk. Ask him or her to instantly say your name every time you use a filler. For some of us, the filler habit is so ingrained that we will not even notice it when it is pointed out to us. It helps to work with a friend who is trying to get rid of his or her own filler habit so you can trade off.

Practice the pause. When you feel tempted to lapse into a filler, just pause. Let it hover lightly in the air—three, four, five, six seconds, or even more—while you gather your thoughts for the next sentence. Push your pauses to the limit. Then get feedback on your pauses: Did they seem forced or nat-ural? Did they heighten the drama of your message and grab your listeners' attention? Remember the disparity that you will feel. It is valuable to get this experience of disparity many times over. You'll be surprised to discover how natural and confident you sound when you have learned the power of the pause.

---

1. Calvin Miller, "Clichés," *SBC LIFE,* June/July 1999, 21.

CHAPTER 17
Skill Seven: Humor

Objective: to use humor to create a bond with your listeners

Humor creates a special bond between you and your listeners. It's virtually impossible to dislike someone who makes us laugh, who helps us enjoy ourselves. We are able to accept tough truths and even correction when they are presented with a light touch. We not only tend to like to be around those people with a sense of humor who can laugh at themselves and the world around them, we tend to trust them more than the grim and serious. A sense of humor—whether sharp and explosive or dry and witty—makes you appear more genial, warmer, and more likable. And the strong, pleasurable emotions people associate with good fun and high spirits make your message enjoyable to listen to—and memorable.

One of the greatest examples of humor in action comes from American political history. In 1984, running for a second term in the White House against Walter Mondale, 76-year-old Ronald Reagan knew that age was a concern in the campaign. If reelected, he would be the oldest president in American history. A fumbling performance against Mondale in the first debate had already created the impression that Reagan was getting a little foggy, if not senile.

So when a reporter served up the age question to Reagan during the second debate, the president was ready for it. "I will not make age an issue of this campaign," he replied with a mischievous glint in his eye. "I am not going to exploit for political purposes my opponent's youth and inexperience." The press and the audience howled. Mondale himself could not repress an unexpected laugh—even though his fate was perhaps sealed at that moment.

The age issue never came up again during the rest of the campaign, and that one exchange was the most remembered event of the debate, arguably of the entire campaign.

———————

Humor can be a powerful tool for packing positive energy into your communication. Your goal and the effect of humor is to make the formal informal. No matter how sticky the situation, humor can turn the tide and make the most reluctant listeners open to your point of view. Though it doesn't come easily, developing an appropriate sense of humor is definitely worth working on.

> *The one who causes them to laugh, gains more votes for the measure than the one who forces them to think.*
> MALCOLM DE CHAZALL

What Others Do

One of the great challenges for a somewhat legalistic and staid Kentucky congregation was that the sanctuary had no air-conditioning to combat the stifling summer heat. Finally the pastor broached the subject during the church business meeting and advocated getting central air installed. The old-timers rose up in arms. This was ungodly, so far as they were concerned, because it was using "worldly enticements" to get people to come to church. The pastor allowed a slight grin to creep across his face. "Then let's take out the furnace," he said. Suddenly the whole church began to laugh, even those who had been so zealous to protect their tradition. The air conditioner was installed shortly thereafter.

John Ralston, formerly a successful NFL football coach, is now a professional speaker. When he just missed taking his team to the national championship, the owner fired him. Shortly after that John was introduced to give a speech with a flowery introduction that forgot to mention what everybody already knew. His opening was: "You know I used to be the coach, but I got fired. I was fired because of illness and fatigue. The fans were sick and tired of me."

Beverly Webb, the founder of a large retail outlet, is a well-known figure in the retail industry. She is also a wife and mother of two children. She was once asked at a news conference whether she would serve as a director on another company's board. Her reply was: "I don't do boards or windows."

Sunny Robbins has a mother in a nursing home whom she calls daily. One of her goals is to do something to make her mother laugh in every phone call. She always is able to succeed.

What You Can Do

Don't tell jokes

First and surprisingly, we strongly say, don't tell jokes! Leave comedy to the comedians. Not many people are really good joke-tellers—perhaps one person in a hundred—and unfortunately, about ten times that many think they are good joke-tellers. If your joke falls flat, you'll go down with it. Everyone in the room feels uncomfortable and embarrassed when a speaker's joke does the old lead balloon. Feeling brains snap shut. Your listeners notice your technique—or lack thereof—rather than your subject matter. Unless you are in that rare 99th percentile who can actually tell a joke successfully, with timing, delivery, and flair, don't.

Second, understand that fun is better than funny. Your goal is not comedy but connection—creating an atmosphere of fun, friendliness, and openness. You want to put your listeners at ease, not develop a comedy routine for a night at the Improv.

Find humor that works for you

So if jokes won't work for you, what will? Perhaps you can use stories and anecdotes. Or perhaps a slightly skewed outlook on life. Of course, a warm, genuine smile always works. Seeing the absurdity of your own world is a good start. What's your sense of humor like? A dry, subtle wit? The ability to poke gentle fun at yourself, to not take yourself too seriously? A unique outlook on everyday life? Do you find unexpected amusement in the things that happen around your home or the office? What kinds of things do you do and say in private conversations that make people laugh and how can you work them into your talk, teaching, preaching, or presentations? Do you have a gift for seeing the humor and the opportunity in a crisis? Use what God has given you—as he has given all of us a sense of humor with different ways to apply it.

Use the humor in language

The right emphasis of a single word can provoke a laugh and cement the connection between you and your listener. Example: the speaker who defined "ageism" as "prejudice against the aged by the temporarily young." The great African-American pastor Shadrach Meshach Lockridge jokes that his mother did not give him the name of the third of the Hebrew children, Abednego, because in those days before improved civil rights she feared that someone might mistakenly call him "a bad Negro."

Think funny

How do you develop humor for your communication? Humor is the hardest communication skill to exercise, and the best exercise is actually working at a mind-set. Think funny, and you will begin to not only see the humor around you, but you will begin to use humor in communication. Look for the humor in the serious—it's almost always there. There is even appropriate laughter and warm memories at funerals. People like to laugh. They like to be with lighthearted people. So do you. Look at those who make you laugh or feel lighthearted, and emulate them.

> Laughter is the shortest distance between two people.
> VICTOR BORGE

Think friendly

This is also a mind-set, and you can exercise your attitude on this one. The next person you see, think of being friendly, rather than judging or advocating or questioning or however you might set your attitude. With this mind-set, humor and humanization are much more likely to occur, and it will become a habit.

Keep a humor notebook

Keep a journal or diary of observations and funny quotations, anecdotes, and stories—especially stories that happen to you. You don't need to write the entire story down—just a few trigger words to bring it back to mind when you're preparing your talk. Review it regularly, and it will add to your mind-set of thinking funny.

CHAPTER 18

Skill Eight: Listener Involvement

Objective: to maintain active interest and involvement of each person to whom you are communicating—whether one person or a thousand

Books dispense information, but human beings communicate. There's a big difference. The question is: Are you a human being or a book? Every time you communicate with another human being via the spoken word, you are doing much more than imparting information. You are revealing ideas, opinions, and emotions. As a Christian communicator committed to sharing the Word, your subject matter and intent is even more significant. You are attempting to move that person to action, or persuade that person to submit to God's Word. In other words, you are trying to involve your listener. If all you want to do is impart information, you might as well be a book!

Right now, we are coming to you in the form of a book. You can read *us*, but we can't read *you*. Are you bored? Fascinated? Irritated? Yawning? Excited? Are you smiling? Frowning? Giving half your attention to the TV? Are you sitting in a comfortable chair? Lying down? Do you sit at a desk and study this book intently, or is it bathroom reading? We don't know! We can't see you and adjust our message to better involve you! At this moment in your life, we are nothing but words on paper!

But if we were sitting together in conversation in your living room, or if you were in our audience—even if you were just one face in a sea of faces—we could involve you in a conversation. We could see if you are falling asleep or leaning forward in anticipation, and we could adjust the message and behavior accordingly. We could change strategy to keep your feeling brain open to the flow of the message.

What Others Do

Contrast

Elisabeth Elliot addressed a group of college students at a gathering sponsored by a well-known campus ministry. Though separated by a generation and years of painful experience, her passionate delivery and "in-your-face" challenge to the tens of thousands of young adults was right on the mark. ". . . have the courage" she said slowly and deliberately, "to stay . . . out . . . of bed."

> *Your listeners won't care how much you know until they know how much you care.*
> ANONYMOUS

At one point in the speech she involved her audience by taking the tone of a "valley girl" and offering feeble excuses such as an ambivalent teen might propose. The effect was electric! Through identifying with her listeners, she had involved them and made them really hear her message.

Dramatic volume

John Rogers was asked to give a talk to a church group. His subject was "Conflict." As he stood up in front of the group, the babble of various conversations continued from different portions of the audience. "Shut up!" John shouted at the top of his lungs. "I'm tired of listening to you! From now on I talk and *you* listen!" At that moment, all eyes—some of them as big as saucers—were looking at John. You could have heard a snowflake drop. John went on: "The man who shouted those words in my face was about six feet tall and two hundred pounds. At that moment, I knew I was in for a heap of conflict." The tension broke, but John's listeners stayed quietly, attentively involved for the rest of his talk.

Using another medium

Rick Warren is the only pastor that Saddleback Valley Community Church has ever had. Taking the church from its inception to its current location and membership of more than fifteen thousand has been largely due to his emphasis on application in his teaching. Warren does many things well, and is consistent in using one simple method of getting his congregation involved in his messages: he includes fill-in-the-blank outlines in the church bulletin. As Warren preaches, his parishioners fill in the key words that complete the application points Warren sees in the biblical text. This simple involving technique is a great tool for learning—and listening.

People as props

Adrian Rogers wanted the members of Bellevue Baptist Church to understand their mission, so right in the middle of his sermon he invited four men in the congregation to come to the platform with him. He placed one at the far left of the platform, one at the far right, and one in the middle, keeping the fourth man by his side. He explained that the man on the left represented the worst sinner who ever lived. Taking advantage of the obvious humor in bestowing such a title on one of his church members, Dr. Rogers explained that the apostle Paul said that was his place, as the "chief of sinners." The man on the far right represented the best Christian in the world. After having a little fun with that, the pastor then explained that the man in the middle represented Jesus Christ. He went on to remind his listeners that everyone they meet is somewhere in that continuum, somewhere between the worst and the best, and more importantly, on one side of Christ or the other. Then taking the fourth man, he placed him between the "worst" and "Jesus." He told the members, "You may not be able to get this man to Jesus, but through your smile and influence, your words and witness, maybe you can move him a step closer. Then one day he comes to know Christ," and with that he moved the subject to the other side of "Jesus," toward the "best man." Then, looking quizzically at the audience he asked, "Are we through with him now?" The entire congregation answered in unison a vibrant, "No!" "No, we aren't!" he assured them. "We want to move him on up the line. That is what discipleship and Bible study is all about!"

What You Can Do

Here are some of the many ideas to involve your audience. Some of them are behaviors we talked about before—here with an added reason for mastery. Use your creativity to mix and combine these in your communication. It takes practice and confidence to risk implementing these, but the reward in your impact is worth every bit of it.

Use drama

You can immediately involve your listener with a strong opening. Start with a striking statement, a dramatic story, or a question that forces the listener to focus on your message. Make your message visual and energetic with the use of action and motion. Create drama with your voice, vocal tone or pitch variation, dramatic pauses, and strong emotional content (anger, sorrow, joy, laughter). Close your talk with a motivational call to specific action or with a memorable quotation.

Maintain eye communication

Don't look over the heads of your audience; meet your listeners in the eye! Survey them for a few moments before you begin speaking. Maintain three to six seconds of eye contact with as many individuals as possible. Don't forget to include people in the "fringes" at either end of the audience or conference table. Read the eye contact they give back to you. Gauge whether your listeners are bored, wary, hostile, interested, or enthusiastic—and adjust your approach accordingly.

Move

Don't nail your shoes to the carpet—move! Avoid using a lectern or hiding behind a pulpit. If a lectern is provided, move out from behind it. Make your movements purposeful and authoritative. Never back away from your audience—it makes you look intimidated. In fact, at both the beginning and end of your talk, it lends force to your message to take a few steps toward your listeners.

Use visuals

In addition to making your own presence as interesting as possible, give your listeners something visual. Make your communication memorable with the use of bold, striking graphic aids, props, overheads, flip charts, or other sensory enhancements if possible and appropriate. Mix assorted kinds of media (for example, use both overheads and video clips) in order to keep the visual dimension varied and interesting. Rehearse the visual part of your presentation so that transitions will be fluid rather than fumbling. Involve your listeners with your visuals; for example, ask questions of your audience and briefly tabulate their answers on an overhead transparency.

Ask questions

Rhetorical questions will keep your listeners thinking and focused. Asking for a volunteer is even more involving. You actually feel a surge of intensity go through an audience, and you can read the thoughts of many of your listeners right on their faces: "Should I answer that question?" Asking for a show of hands also generates involvement and gives you a quick gauge of your audience's mood and opinions.

Use demonstrations

Plan and time every step or procedure. Have a volunteer from the audience assist in the demonstration. Above all, make sure your demonstration *works*. Nothing is more disheartening or distracting than an ill-prepared or poorly executed demonstration that backfires. Get rid of all the variables so you are certain that the audience gets your intended point.

Once a pastor wanted to illustrate the incredible pressure on marriages and how one small matter can bring the whole marriage down. He had seen teenage boys stand on empty pop cans in the parking lot, amazed that they would hold the entire weight of a two-hundred-pound man standing flat-footed on top of the can. Then someone else would take a pen or some small object and lightly touch the side of the can bearing the human weight. The can would then be crushed flat beneath the load it was bearing. Thinking it a fitting illustration, the pastor asked for a volunteer from the audience to come to the platform, intending to use the subject to illustrate his point. He had never tried the scenario on the platform, however, and did not realize that a spongy carpeted surface made it impossible to distribute weight flatly on top. When his volunteer crushed the can immediately, even before he could touch the side with a pen or explain his point, he didn't have a backup can for a clumsy second effort. People would not remember his point but his embarrassment. The lesson is simple: When you demonstrate a concept for your listeners, make sure the demonstration doesn't backfire!

Use samples and gimmicks

Have fun with your listeners. If appropriate to your subject matter, have samples or small gifts available to give as rewards for volunteer participants. Be creative with using gimmicks, but be careful. Gimmicks can backfire, so proceed with caution. When they work well, they work very well. But when they bomb, they explode with a big bang.

Create interest

Remember that your listeners have a short attention span. Pace your various involvement techniques to keep the level of interest high. Use eye contact to gauge your listeners' involvement.

Dr. D. James Kennedy, pastor of Coral Ridge Presbyterian Church in Fort Lauderdale, Florida, got his church's and television audience's attention when he announced one Sunday morning that a large amount of money was missing from the church coffers. A hush immediately fell on a shocked congregation as he spent several minutes expressing his own incredulity that anyone would dare to steal God's money. He confessed that he was innocent and that his conscience was clear in the matter, but that God knew and would eventually judge whoever was guilty. Then he further explained that the missing money of which he spoke was not money that had been donated to the church and then embezzled or mismanaged. The missing money that some guilty party possessed was tithes that had never been given, God's command notwithstanding. Then he launched into his exposition of Malachi 3:8: "'Will a man rob God?'" He had his listeners' attention and interest the rest of the sermon!

Most of all, keep your own interest level high, even if you are giving a familiar speech, lesson, or sermon for the thousandth time. Change the order, change techniques, vary the stories you use. If you demonstrate genuine enthusiasm for your message, your emotional involvement and energy will be infectious!

CHAPTER 19
Skill Nine: The Natural Self

Objective: to be authentic, learning new skills so they become natural

The natural self is a paradox. It is the most simple "skill"—to be yourself is easy and obviously natural. Yet so often we are unconscious about how that "self" comes across to others. Often that self is not natural, but is nervous or uncomfortable and not the way God intended us to be. And we usually don't know it. So the difficult part comes from gaining conscious awareness of how we come across, and then learning new skills so we can have conscious choice about our impact on others.

Being our natural self is being authentic and gaining the skills of communication so they become part of us. It is moving from the stage of unconscious incompetence to unconscious competence (see Maslow's stages on page 104–105). It is taking a look at our natural and unnatural habits and getting a choice about them.

WHAT OTHERS DO

A fictional story

In an isolated area of Italy, there is a small town surrounded by mountains with craggy cliffs and caves. People moved into these caves and over time were looked on with disdain by the town dwellers. The hermit "cave colony" did no harm. They lived by themselves in isolated and primitive circumstances.

One year, a cruel young man named Saul began work at the town foundry. He organized a gang that regularly harassed the cave people. After a few years of abuse, something unusual happened. On a quiet Sunday morning, a cave dweller named Pietro came down from the hills. He calmly walked to the town square and began speaking. He was dressed in shabby clothes. He did not have formal schooling or social grace. But he talked with confidence and conviction. A crowd gathered. He asked why the peaceful cave dwellers were being persecuted. He described their lives in the cave, and the unhappiness caused by Saul and his gang. Although Pietro had a simple vocabulary, he held the crowd enthralled with his message. He spoke confidently, as he spoke from his heart. He was a natural. From that day forward, the harassment ceased, as the townspeople forced Saul to stop his bullying.

> *When we encounter a natural style we are always surprised and delighted, for we thought to see an author, and found a man.*
> BLAISE PASCAL

A true story

> Then Peter, filled with the Holy Spirit, said to them: "Rulers and elders of the people! If we are being called to account today for an act of kindness shown to a cripple and are asked how he was healed, then know this, you and all the people of Israel: It is by the name of Jesus Christ of Nazareth, whom you crucified but whom God raised from the dead, that this man stands before you healed. He is 'the stone you builders rejected, which has become the capstone.' Salvation is found in no one else, for there is no other name under heaven given to men by which we must be saved." When they saw the courage of Peter and John and realized that they were unschooled, ordinary men, they were astonished and they took note that these men had been with Jesus. (Acts 4:8–13)

WHAT YOU CAN DO

Use habits wisely

God made us to use habits constructively. We have literally hundreds, even thousands of habits that help us daily, so that we do not have to bring everything up to conscious thought. We can dress, drive, and dine without thinking. Can you imagine what it would be like if you had to think of what arm to put in your shirt first when you dress, or how to lift your leg to apply the brakes when you drive, or what you need to do to put your fork into a piece of food? We need to do many things at the subconscious level, but we do not need to communicate at the unconscious level. We are creatures of habits in communication as well, and what this book is about is to bring those habits to the conscious level so we can have some choice about our communication habits. You are not born with your communication habits—they are developed.

In his book *Psycho-Cybernetics*, Maxwell Maltz said that it takes twenty-one days to change a habit, and our experience shows that he is about right. There are hundreds of interpersonal communication habits that we have, both positive and negative. Most are in the nine communication skill areas covered in this book. Changing habits takes practice—framing, forming, and molding our minds to do certain physical behaviors that are repeated over and over again.

Change habits that are not working

To make a forward lean and increase your habit-changing skills, change one communication habit a day. Work on them regularly. Today concentrate on eye communication—looking at people for five seconds at a time. Tomorrow concentrate on replacing nonwords with a pause. Use audio feedback with your voice mail. One day try to consciously overdo your gestures. (You probably can't.) Or roller coaster your voice.

The four stages of learning

The psychologist who gave us the "Hierarchy of Needs," Abraham Maslow, also has given us a valuable framework to understand how we learn anything, which he called the "Four Stages of Learning." This is a useful concept when you are looking at changing habits.

1. Unconscious Incompetence—We *don't know* that we don't know. Most of us who have never had extensive feedback about our interpersonal skills are at this state of unconscious incompetence. We are not aware of our interpersonal communication habits.

2. Conscious Incompetence—We *know* that we don't know. Here we learn that we are not competent at something. This often comes as a rude awakening, usually through feedback. Video feedback is particularly valuable in moving us from stage 1 to stage 2.

3. Conscious Competence—We *consciously work* at what we don't know. We make an effort to learn a new skill. Practice, drill, and repetition are at the forefront. This is where most learning takes place. It takes effort and work.

4. Unconscious Competence—We *don't have to think* about knowing it. The skill set happens automatically at an unconscious level. A speaker with a distracting habit who has learned to overcome it through practice doesn't have to concentrate on *not* doing the distracting habit.

Consider the juggler

Every juggler first starts with one ball, just to get the rhythm, then adds another to practice with both hands working together. Finally, a third ball is added, and more, until the juggler juggles proficiently. Becoming an expert in interpersonal communications is much like juggling. You master one skill at a time and add to them once they become a habit.

Start by acknowledging your natural strengths and be thankful you don't have to learn them from scratch, for many others do. You may have an easy, natural smile, while others may have to work at relaxing in their interpersonal communications. On the other hand, you may find it difficult to gesture naturally, but another might have been born more effusive. Acknowledge strengths and work to improve and capitalize on them.

Then work on your weaknesses, one at a time, until they become strengths. Take your weakest area first and concentrate on improving it every day for a week. Using "um" and "ah" may be a difficulty for you. Put your conscious mental energy into leaving pauses each day for a week or two—with no nonwords! Then move to another skill. Continue that process until you have gone through the many parts of all nine skills.

COMMUNICATING WELL IS A LIFETIME PROCESS

We are not born effective communicators. God gave us certain potentials and abilities and much room to learn and to change. He gave us habits to help us in all things and particularly in communication. We always find new unwanted habits that pop up, as well as old undesirable habits that creep back in. We also find new strengths as we mature and experiment with various behavioral skills. Often synergy occurs where a new-found habit will improve an old habit. Or two habits work together to form an effective new behavior. For example, movement and extended eye communication can breed confidence that allows somebody to maintain excellent eye communication with an individual and even allows a reaching out and touching the arm of the listener.

Don't expect to ever arrive at some high plateau of perfect communication. You will always have room for improvement, areas that demand concentration and work. But though you may not arrive, you will definitely be on the right path, and you will have the right tools to continue your progress and growth as an effective communicator whom God can and will use.

Part V
The Content Skills

OK, we've learned to establish trust with the listener. We're natural. We can leave pauses and use gestures and smile. We can connect with people. Now let's put together our content. Let's spend a lot of time in technical research and carefully analyze how we are going to put together a really good message and get it just right. Let's craft it and write it out and read it so we are sure not to miss anything, then we'll have the whole package, right?

Wrong!

Don't ruin the good connection you've made with people by clamping down on your energy and inventiveness when it comes to creating and delivering your content. Don't pay so much attention to the precise words that you lose sight of your audience and your purpose.

We often ask in seminars what's more important, style or substance. And of course the answer is—yes!

You have to have *both* to be effective. Up to this point we've concentrated on your style—how you come across as a presenter. Now it's time for the other half of the equation—to create what you are going to say.

CHAPTER 20

Using the Communication Channel

Repeatedly, we see three basic problems in the majority of people giving speeches, presentations, and sermons. We also find them in meetings, at the other end of phone conversations, and even on voice mail.

Take a look at the following communication situations and see if you haven't found yourself caught in these circumstances too many times:

The Borer may be well researched and even clear. He may share a lot of good information, facts, and data. He may appear logical, serious, earnest and sincere and may even have a point and yet . . . He is so boring as he drones on and on in a monotone. You have lost interest or have fallen asleep, and at best there is certainly minimum impact even if you paid attention while he was getting to his point.

Words, Words, Words,
Words, Words, Words,
Words, Words, Words,
Words, Words, Words,
Words, Words, Words,
Words, Words, Words,
Words, Words, Words,
Words, Words, Words,
Words, Words, Words,
Words, Words, Words,
Words, Words, Words,
Words..............*Point*

BORING

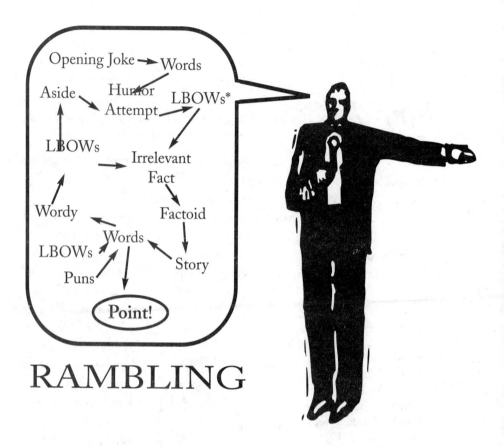

RAMBLING

* LBOWs = "lovely bunch of words

The Rambler may not talk in a monotone, and will get you laughing, and even has a point, but, boy, he takes a long time in getting there. And by the time he does you wonder whether the trip was worth it.

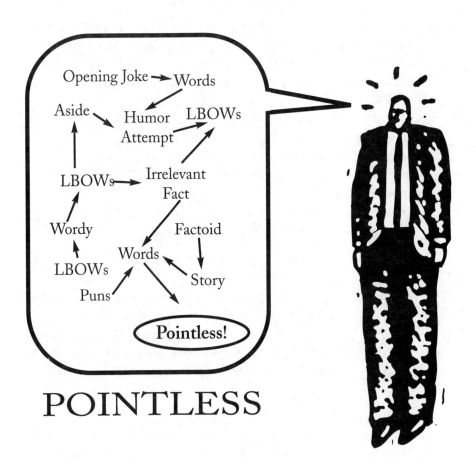

POINTLESS

The worst problem of all is the rambler who has no point at all, and though the trip might have been a diversion, it sure wasn't worth it.

Beware the LBOWs

How often we see bluster and braggadocio in so much communication, usually as people air their own opinions. Sometimes we hear a lot of words that don't really say anything. We call these LBOWs or "lovely bunch of words." The LBOW is when someone says something that sounds good, but means very little. I'll give an example.

> "I'm here to talk to you today, and I want to talk on a subject that is familiar to all of us. It's an area that I've done a lot of research on, and is an area that we all have an interest in I think. I'm glad to be here. I've enjoyed my preliminary talks with many of you, and so I hope that you will enjoy my remarks as I've enjoyed putting them together. And I think that it will be valuable to us all. So in my talk this evening. . . ."

> *A fool finds no pleasure in understanding but delights in airing his own opinions.*
> PROVERBS 18:2

A lovely bunch of words that sounds fine but doesn't say anything. They are like "a resounding gong or a clanging cymbal." Signifying nothing. The speaker who gets results is the one who first listens to God's wisdom. She is focused in her message, with a strong point of view and a listener-based message. She clearly describes the benefits to her audience.

It's Not Print

So that's where you want to go. To fully use the spoken communication channel to its maximum benefit, remember that it's not print. The difference between the written and spoken word is vast. When you want to get across information, do it in print. But when you want to create action, speak.

Combine your conviction and content with energetic and authentic delivery. You want to use this powerful spoken communication channel in the right way. To move people. To teach. To motivate. To share how Jesus Christ has changed your life.

So don't go back and write out a speech! Don't get up and read a speech! There is a better way.

CHAPTER 21
Putting Water in the Pipe

Think of the communication channel as a pipe designed to carry pure water. The pipe is built, waiting for that crystal clear cool water. How do you best purify that water that you are about to put in the pipe?

You ARE THE CONTENT

It's not the medium that's the message. *You* are the message.

First, you are the message by being authentic. What you do (in communicating) speaks so loudly people begin to get the message before they hear the words you say. You connect with people with confidence so they are ready and willing to hear what you say. That is when the listener really hears your content.

And you are also your content. Your life experiences. Your changed life in Christ. Your knowledge. Your opinions and perspective and experience and wisdom. Up to this point we have focused on style and delivery. If you think of behavior as the pipe, your content is the water that fills that pipe. You are putting your words and ideas and advocacy into the pipe, and you want that water (content) to be as pure and as nourishing as you can make it.

There is a way to prepare that achieves your objective.

WISDOM AND PREPARATION

The biblical principle behind your content is contained in Proverbs 13:15: "Good understanding wins favor." When we understand what we want to accomplish, what our listeners need to know, and the benefits for them, we win favor with our audience.

Some people love to wing it in life, particularly in communication. Many don't like to rehearse or be prepared. That is not only a mistake in the practical sense, but it is counter to what God would have us do.

DIRECTION

Proverbs 21:31 teaches that preparation is key: "The horse is made ready for the day of battle, but victory rests with the LORD." We get our horses ready—we prepare and train the army, but the victory rests with the Lord. We prepare ourselves and our messages and our ideas, then allow the Lord to flow through us. He wants us to succeed when we are communicating the right things, and he will empower us to be more effective.

Listen to these inspiring verses from Proverbs that reinforce this. From chapter 16, verse 1: "To man belong the plans of the heart, but from the LORD comes the reply of the tongue." And Proverbs 20:18 echoes, "Make plans by seeking advice; if you wage war, obtain guidance."

THE ULTIMATE PURIFIER

Ultimately, we realize as in Proverbs 16:23: "A wise man's heart guides his mouth, and his lips promote instruction." Where does the wise man's direction come from? Proverbs 21:1 answers, "The king's heart is in the hand of the LORD; he directs it like a watercourse wherever he pleases."

Isn't it great that we have a sovereign God, who can direct our watercourse wherever he pleases? He will give us pure water, if we let him. He is wisdom, and we can trust him to direct us toward the greatest benefit to all.

CHAPTER 22
An Exercise

Content often gets in the way of process because we get so wrapped up in what we want to say that we forget the process that gets us there. If we're going to let God work through us, we have to get out of the way. We must flow rather than restrict.

Our experience is not unlike that of an athlete—perhaps a basketball player shooting a foul shot with the game tied and a second on the clock. He is concentrating more on the importance of the shot going in—the content—than on the process of how he is going to put it in. This is the very situation he works on continuously in practice.

Perhaps we are more like the contractor. He is thinking only about the process of building the pipeline, not the quality of the water that will flow into it when the work is done. That will come later.

So think of these next few chapters as practice—the process of putting your creative ideas together and delivering them—without thinking of the importance of the ideas themselves—the water in the pipe.

THINK OF A SUBJECT

To get you away from thinking about content, we are going to take you through an exercise in which the subject is not about life, faith, wisdom, work, or anything weighty—but a hobby, sport, or activity that you are passionate about.

Your Subject

Think of a subject like that and write it down on a piece of paper or Post-it note. Then conjure up what you might say about it if you had someone sitting across from you and you had to give a little talk.

When we ask seminar participants to do this exercise, the minitalks that each person gives to his or her partner are often short, unfocused, and rambling.

For our demonstration example we're going to take the subject of golf. The ideas for a minitalk might look like this:

- Golf is very popular.
- I play it whenever I can.
- Tiger Woods has really popularized it.
- My wife doesn't like it particularly.
- I have a friend, though, whose wife is separating to try the pro circuit.
- It is sometimes boring to watch, but I saw Tiger at the Masters.
- The country club isn't too expensive.

At this stage the ideas seem short, unfocused, and rambling. How can you improve the process?

1. What's your point?

What are you trying to accomplish with this talk? How do you feel about golf? Good, bad, or indifferent? If you're indifferent, you shouldn't be talking about it anyway.

But you feel passionate about the subject. You love the game! And so your point is that golf is good, and everybody should take it up because there's much to learn from it and it's great relaxation.

But someone else may have the opposite point of view. Golf is bad, a waste of good time, hurts marriage relationships, and shouldn't be encouraged in company outings, etc. You can see how a different point of view would change the entire presentation.

But your point of view is clear and personal. By focusing on your point of view, you begin to only talk about those things that will promote that point of view. Your mind consistently attracts to it only those things that will help your cause, as long as you feel passionate about that cause.

So in your golf talk, take the positive point of view and capture it with the following few words:

Golf is a sport with great value

Write your point of view (POV) on your subject in this box. Just write a few words to describe how you feel about your subject:

Your POV

2. Whom are you talking to?

You first want to be focused and sure of what you're trying to accomplish, then you want to know whom you're talking to. How much do your listeners know about the subject? Are they for it or against it? Are they for or against you? What's their attitude? What does the group demographic look like?

So for your golf talk, imagine you're in a communications training class with people who live in a large city. They are:

- *About half male and female/ upper socioeconomic background*
- *Either favorable or hostile to the subject, but not neutral*
- *Favorable to me*

Think of a specific audience to whom you might present your subject and jot down a few comments here:

Your Specific Audience

3. What do you want your audience to do?

Usually when you're talking, you don't automatically think of an action step for your listeners. But if you're speaking rather than chatting, feel passionate about the subject, and have a point of view, shouldn't you want them to *do* something? You bet!

With golf as your subject, your general objective would be to get others to play golf. But to persuade them to adopt your viewpoint, make a specific action plan. You might advocate:

Sign up for the free lesson I've arranged at nearby driving range

Write your specific action step(s) for your audience:

Action Step

4. What's the benefit for listeners?

What's in it for them—the audience? Too often we focus on the benefits for ourselves, and to be effective we have to reverse that. If your listeners don't see the benefits for them, they will be unlikely to take your action step, and your purpose will not be met.

So in the golf example, the benefits to your audience might be:

Learn a new skill

Build relationships

Recreation and relaxation

What would be three benefits for your audience if they were to buy into your POV and take your action step? Write them here:

Benefit

Benefit

Benefit

LAYING THE CORNERSTONES

You've just built a foundation for a clear, focused talk on your subject. If we were to summarize your talk as we did at the outset, it might look like this:

POV: Golf is a sport with great value.

Action Step: I have a free opportunity for you to play.

Benefits: For a new skill, building relationships, and fun.

If you had to talk on the subject of golf, your thoughts might go like this:

- Golf is a great game, great value.
- I've only been playing for a few years.
- Shot a hole in one—great thrill.
- My kids are playing, and we hope to make it a family adventure.
- We watched the Masters together; Tiger Woods inspired us all.
- Golf has also built relationships in which I can share my faith with others.
- Once I made a business sale of more than $25,000 on a golf course.
- The outdoors, the fresh air, and walking are great even when I don't play well.
- If you don't play, would you come with me to the driving range?
- It's a great game. Let's play together—I have a free spot in a foursome!

Now take your subject and write down the key words from your POV, action steps, and benefits here:

Your POV

Your Action Step(s)

Benefits to your audience

Now imagine giving your talk to the same person on the same subject as you did several minutes ago. Wouldn't the focus and ability to present many more ideas in a cogent and confident manner have increased dramatically? Actually do it out loud if you can, and see what happens!

In seminars when we do this exercise and people have done the cornerstones like this, then take that same subject they talked about the first time and talk about it again, the results are amazing. The second minitalks are more focused, energetic, confident, interesting, and longer. The energy in the room doubles. All from a simple, ten-minute exercise. If people can do that with a hobby, think of what they can do with something of importance and with more time to prepare.

What We've Just Done

In this exercise we have just done the cornerstones step, the first of four steps in the Decker Grid System. In the next few chapters we will take you through the grid in specific detail so you will be able to prepare all of your messages and speeches with this useful tool. It will not only ensure that you have listener-based, focused messages, but it can cut your preparation time in half, and unleash your creativity.

Opposing View

You can also use the cornerstones to produce a focused message of exactly the opposite view. Let's assume that you thought golf was bad. Your cornerstones might look like this:

1. What's your point?

Golf is bad and should be discouraged as a leisure activity.

2. Who am I talking to?

Let's say you're the COO of a medium-sized ministry, and you're talking to all the management team members. They are mostly middle-aged men who like golf. They are favorable to golf and favorable to you but not favorable to your point of view that golf is "bad."

3. What do you want your listeners to do?

Your general objective would be to lessen their interest and time spent in playing the game. You want to encourage them to find a different activity. Specifically with this group your action step would be rather than take a golfing vacation this year, sign up for the Family Camp Week that the local conference center is starting this year.

4. What's the benefit for them?

Point out the benefits of fun in new and different activities, better family relationships, and support for a good cause.

Now your talk would be filled with ideas that support these cornerstones and be just as focused, energetic, confident, interesting, and longer with a completely different purpose.

CHAPTER 23
The Decker Grid System

Many messages, presentations, conversations, sermons, and teachings are often boring, rambling, or pointless, but the Decker Grid System almost guarantees you won't have those problems. It forces you to have a listener-based message and encourages spontaneity and the human touch in your content. In addition, it allows you to create your messages in about half the time.

THE SYSTEM ITSELF

In the next several chapters we are going to take you through the Decker Grid System in an interactive way so you will be able to use it in real life. We urge you to do the exercises and not just read through them. Then test the process in your real life.

It can change your life if presenting yourself and your ideas is important. And of course it is—since God has commanded us.

> *Give us the tools, and we will finish the job.*
> WINSTON CHURCHILL

CREATING MESSAGES THAT MOTIVATE

The grid is a four-part process that will help you create messages that motivate. It is based on the way the mind actually works—quickly and spontaneously. It uses three basic concepts or tools:

1. Trigger Words

When you prepare a spoken message, don't write out sentences. Use trigger words instead. You are far more efficient when you create with building blocks, each one made up of the concepts and ideas you wish to communicate. These building blocks, or trigger words, prompt the wealth of working knowledge within your mind—ideas, facts, stories, etc. You can think of them as file names or key words within files.

A trigger word is the shortest word, group of words, or symbol about which you could talk for thirty seconds to five minutes.

2. Grid message molders

In the following pages you will be using message folders designed for the Decker Grid System. They are also used separately so each speech or message can be created, delivered, and saved. Trigger words are used with the message folders in the four-step grid process.

3. Post-it Notes

The trigger words are jotted on these familiar sticky notes. Your notes will move around, and so the Post-it notes work much better than the often used 3 x 5-inch cards or notepads. You won't use all of your ideas. The ones that are used could end up in any order. Post-it notes allow you to shuffle ideas around quickly, sorting and discarding them, until you finally arrange them for maximum clarity and impact. The Decker Grid System prompts you through this activity so that in no time flat you achieve order from chaos.

Post-its "Upside Down"

When you use Post-its in the Decker Grid System, place them "upside down" with the sticky portion at the bottom. Post-its (or similar notes) are usually used with the sticky portion at the top, but this allows the bottoms of the notes to curl up away from you, and they are more difficult to read when you are using them as notes. When you start with them "upside down," they will curl toward you as you lay the sheet of paper down on a table or lectern for your notes. (And remember to use the small 1 1/2 x 2-inch Post-its. Not only does that size fit the system, but that will encourage you to be sparing in jotting down your "trigger words.")

THE FOUR-STEP PROCESS

The four-step grid system is simple in execution and profound in impact. It takes common sense ideas and puts them together in a different way. Here are the four basic steps:

The Decker Grid System
1. Cornerstones
2. Create
3. Cluster
4. Compose

1. Cornerstones

When you lay your cornerstones, you create the context for your message. Cornerstones establish the purpose or foundation. They stimulate your thinking and focus your attention on your listener's perspective, what you want your listener to do, and how he/she will benefit.

2. Create

When you create, you unleash your mind's potential to generate ideas to support your subject.

3. Cluster

When you cluster, you group your ideas according to common themes.

4. Compose

When you compose, you organize and edit your clusters. The end result is your best ideas, arranged and ready to be communicated.

CHAPTER 24

Focus: Setting the Cornerstones

The purpose of the Decker Grid System is to help you organize and deliver your ideas in a rapid and memorable manner and to ensure that you are focused in what you want to say and clear in your purpose.

It offers various benefits. You will be on target with any listener or audience, be able to organize your ideas quickly, and develop a new way of thinking.

Begin your work on the following pages. You can use the cornerstones you did in chapter 22, but we suggest you start a new grid on the new template. Here are the instructions:

BUILDING THE CORNERSTONES

1. Pick a subject to talk about, and write it in a word or two on a Post-it note. Place it in the Subject cloud.
2. Think of your point of view. How do you feel about this subject? Define your passion with an active verb.
3. Think of your audience, a specific audience or person, and put that Post-it on the Listener square.
4. Think of the general and specific action steps, and place those two Post-its on the Action Step box.
5. Think of three benefits for the audience and write these in the Benefits box.

1. POV
(Point of View)

Your feeling,
opinion and attitude
about the subject

4. BENEFITS

The Benefits
YOUR LISTENERS
will receive from taking
your Action Step(s).
List three benefits.

2. LISTENERS

1. Who are they?
2. What do they know
   about the subject?
3. How do they feel
   about the subject?

3. ACTION STEP

1. General Action Step
2. Specific Action Step
   (Measurable, realistic,
   specific time frame.)

Cornerstones of the Golf Example

Learn a
new skill

GOLF

Build
Relationships

Golf has
great value

Have
Fun!

Mixed group
Not neutral
Favorable to me

Play
Golf

Sign-up for
free lesson

Delivering the Cornerstones

There will be times when you don't have time to go on to steps 2, 3, and 4 to create, cluster, and compose. Then the cornerstones become more than the beginning tool for structuring your mind. You can actually sequence them and deliver your message from them.

If you are delivering the cornerstones, all you have to do is:

1. State your POV.
2. State your action step.
3. State the benefits.

It's as simple as that. You will want to verbally add and embellish on your cornerstones even as you are speaking, but in effect you have already "memorized" your message and can deliver it in about thirty seconds to five minutes or more if necessary.

Here is the delivery order:

Delivery

POV | Action Steps | Benefits

The Spiritual Cornerstones

The Bible contains many references to communicating (well over four hundred), and many Scripture verses also advocate having a clear and focused message. Here are four specific writings of Paul and James that relate to the four cornerstones:

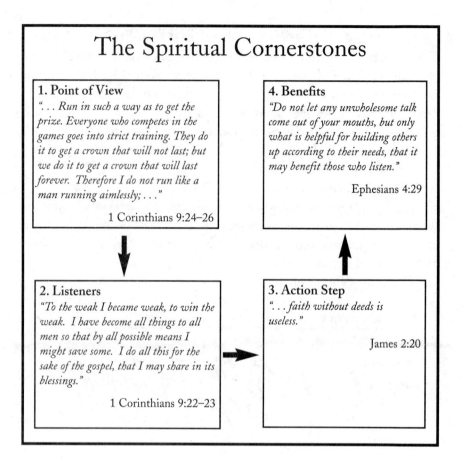

The Spiritual Cornerstones

1. Point of View
". . . Run in such a way as to get the prize. Everyone who competes in the games goes into strict training. They do it to get a crown that will not last; but we do it to get a crown that will last forever. Therefore I do not run like a man running aimlessly; . . ."

1 Corinthians 9:24–26

4. Benefits
"Do not let any unwholesome talk come out of your mouths, but only what is helpful for building others up according to their needs, that it may benefit those who listen."

Ephesians 4:29

2. Listeners
"To the weak I became weak, to win the weak. I have become all things to all men so that by all possible means I might save some. I do all this for the sake of the gospel, that I may share in its blessings."

1 Corinthians 9:22–23

3. Action Step
". . . faith without deeds is useless."

James 2:20

CHAPTER 25
Create, Cluster, and Compose

Remember, the Decker Grid System has four specific steps. The most important step is the cornerstones step, because you have to do that first to determine where you are going. Although you can deliver a short presentation with just the cornerstones, the next three steps of creating your ideas, grouping them, and then organizing and editing them are critical to the complete presentation. Here are the four steps again.

The Decker Grid System
1. Cornerstones
2. Create
3. Cluster
4. Compose

In this chapter we will describe each step, give an example, and provide a working page for you to do a sample interactive exercise on your chosen subject.

CREATE

The purpose of the *create* step is to brainstorm for a few minutes to get as many ideas as possible out on the page, using only a trigger word or two for each Post-it. You do not edit or organize at this stage. You want the first ideas that come to mind that relate to your four cornerstones—facts and figures, stories, data, examples, concepts, etc. Think of as many as you can quickly and put them on the page. After about three minutes you should have about fifteen ideas on your create page, which might look like this:

idea *idea* *idea* *idea*

idea *idea*

idea *idea* *idea*

idea

idea *idea* *idea*

idea *idea* *idea*

The Golf Create Example

Ben Story

Watching Tiger

Discipline

Healthy

Family Relationships

Reflects Life

Focus

Builds Character

Builds Relationships

Can Do Alone

Walking

Slow Learning

Business Bonding

Rules of the Game

Proverbs 13:11

Rules of Life

Exercise

6 a.m. Rounds

Subtle

Pros?

The Tipping Point

Variety of Courses

Practice and Play

Upsets

Rule of Random Reinforcement

Need for Practice

Your Create Example

Now give yourself a time limit of three minutes, really time yourself and work to get at least fifteen trigger words written down on Post-its (upside down!) that relate to your subject—ideas, facts, stories, quotes, numbers, etc. Remember the principles of brainstorming—no censoring or editing here (that comes later). Let one idea trigger another. Your goal is quantity, not quality. Ready, go!

CLUSTER

The purpose of the *cluster* step is to begin the editing process by organizing the random ideas that you brainstormed in the *create* step. Group your ideas naturally, remembering that like attracts like.

Begin by taking an idea and placing it in a corner of the page, then place related ideas with it. Move one of the remaining ideas to another place on the page and cluster similar ideas with that, until you have perhaps three, four, or five, or more clusters. Once you have a theme of what your cluster is about, underline the best "idea" Post-it that describes that cluster, or make a new Post-it that describes that cluster, and that becomes your key point. Here is how it might look:

The Golf Cluster Example

Builds Relationships

Ben Story

Family Relationships

Business Bonding

Fun

Variety of Courses

Upsets

Watching Tiger

Pros?

Healthy

Walking

Exercise

Available

Can Do Alone

6 a.m. Rounds

Discipline

Builds Character

Slow Learning

Example of Tiger

Need For Practice

Focus

Proverbs 13:11

Lessons of Life

Subtle

Rules of Game

Rules of Life

The Tipping Point

Practice and Play

Reflect Life

Rule of Random Reinforcement

Your Cluster Example

Now take about five minutes and cluster the Post-its that you created in step 2: the *create* step. You could transfer them to this page, although it is easier to just do the clustering on the create page itself. Remember that the creating process never ends, and when you think of a new idea, fact, or story, just write it on another Post-it and cluster it. When you are done, your cluster page will look something like this:

COMPOSE

The purpose of the *compose* step is to edit your ideas to keep the best. Keep it simple, using the rule of three. Take your three best key points from the *cluster* step and place them on the compose page, putting them in order of importance, saving the best for last. Then take your best subpoints to each key point and place them under their key points. You should end up with twelve Post-its on the page, looking like this:

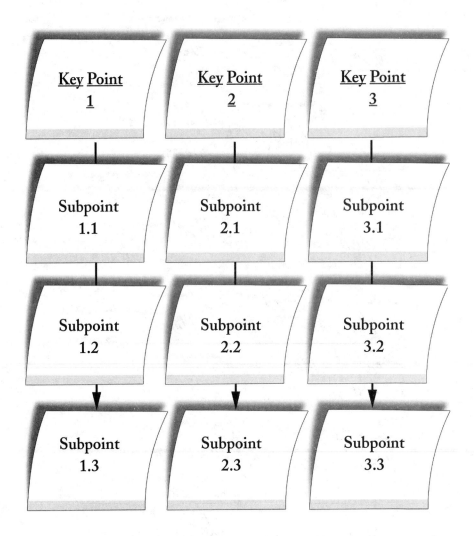

The Golf Compose Example

Builds Relationships	Builds Character	Fun
Ben Story	Discipline	Watching Tiger
Family Relationships	Lessons of Life	Can Do Alone
Business Bonding	Need For Practice	Healthy

Your Compose Example

Take about ten minutes and choose the three best key points from your *cluster* working page and place them in order of importance on the key points sample on this *compose* page. Then take the three best subpoints of each key point and place them. Notice that you will not be able to use all your ideas. That's OK. You want to use the KISS principle—"keep it simple, sweetheart." Less is more. You can always speak any of your ideas when you are talking, but as notes, you just want to have your best ideas on the page to trigger your mind when you need to. You don't want a cluttered page.

After you have the three key points and three subpoints for each, then look again at any of your ideas that you did not use. If any are better than those you have on your final grid, see if you can replace them. You will find that usually an idea left over, or even more so a key point that you didn't use, can fit in and make sense under a different key point. The object is to end up with your best ideas on the page.

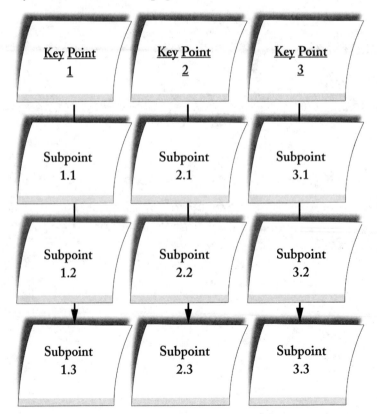

Delivery—With Opening and Closing

When you deliver your grid presentation, you will add a simple opening and closing. This one never fails. Start with a story or quote (SHARP principle; see chapter 27), then state your POV, action step, and second best benefit. (You'll save the best benefit for last.) Then tell your listeners key point 1, then subpoints 1, then key points 2 and subpoints 2, then key points 3 and subpoints 3. Then close by restating your POV, action step, and best benefit. And to end with a flourish, add another SHARP principle. It would look like this:

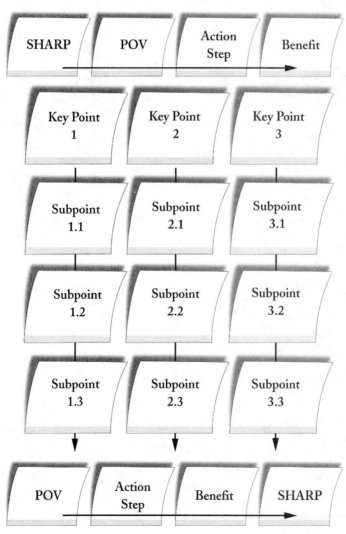

The Golf Delivery Example

Tiger Woods Phenomenon	Golf is Great	Play It	Build Relationships and Have fun

<u>Builds Relationships</u>	<u>Builds Character</u>	*Fun*
Ben Story	Discipline	Watching Tiger
Family Relationships	<u>Lessons of Life</u>	Can do Alone
Business Bonding	Need for Practice	<u>Healthy</u>

Golf is Great	Sign Up for Free Lesson	You'll Learn Life Lessons	LLBTR "Live Life by the Rules"

Your Delivery Example

Now you can either move your grid Post-its that you did in the *compose* step a few pages back onto this page and use this template, or leave the Post-its there and do these final delivery steps on that page a few pages back.

Either way, take these final few minutes to complete your opening and closing. For the opening, place your POV, action steps, and second-best benefit above your completed compose step grid. Add a SHARP at the front end to complete your opening.

For the closing you will then repeat placing new Post-its, duplicating where necessary your POV, action step, and the best benefit at the bottom of your grid, as in the sample. Then choose a final SHARP quote or story to end with, and you will have completed your closing.

Then all that is left is to deliver it. Note the delivery order on page 144.

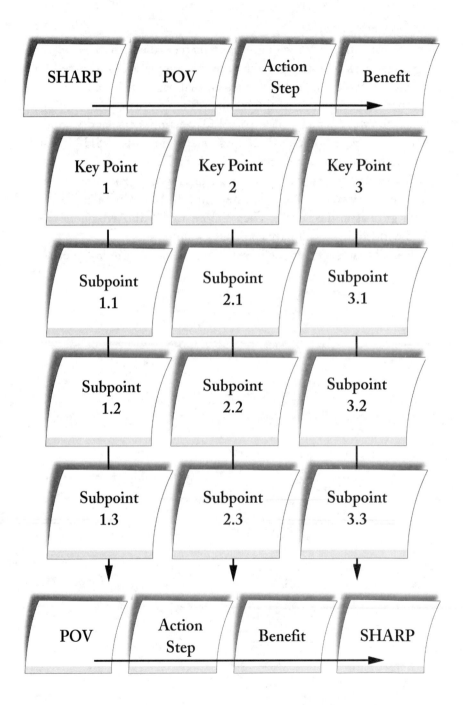

Part VI
Applying Bold Assurance

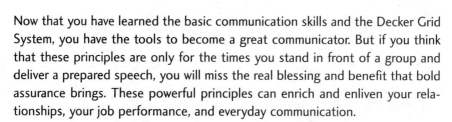

Now that you have learned the basic communication skills and the Decker Grid System, you have the tools to become a great communicator. But if you think that these principles are only for the times you stand in front of a group and deliver a prepared speech, you will miss the real blessing and benefit that bold assurance brings. These powerful principles can enrich and enliven your relationships, your job performance, and everyday communication.

Being a better communicator is at the heart of all the things in life that matter most. God made us and placed us in a social setting. The ability to talk to your spouse in a loving and positive manner or the capability to correct your child in a way that encourages and directs rather than demeans and diminishes her spirit can significantly change the character and quality of your home life. The difference between influencing and alienating your teenager or a coworker usually lies in the way you communicate.

Once you know how to be a feeling-brain communicator, you can get your message across more effectively in all of your life. When you can apply the four cornerstones to the way you present ideas in *any* setting, you will find more comfort and freedom of expression than you ever thought possible. You become a natural, but you have a confidence that is supernatural.

In this final section, open yourself to a range of possibilities. Consider the opportunities to take more of a leadership role in your career and in your church. Look at your life with a forward lean, and God will bless you for your faith.

CHAPTER 26
Speaking from the Heart

We have given you methods of creating content and then delivering that content with a confidence and certainty that will make all of your communications powerful. Our goal is to help you share God's principles for living with others and to impact lives through his Word. We are convinced that God's Word is worthy of our greatest efforts and that such a wonderful subject matter deserves to be delivered with passion, energy, and excitement.

Though changing lives is God's work, he uses human means to effect that change. Certainly God could have chosen any way he wanted to convey his love and to redeem us, but the Bible teaches that it is primarily through the "foolishness of preaching"—personal communication—that God reveals himself.

Bold assurance is the distillation of sound principles that make us available to God for his use. These principles, correctly applied, help us to get ourselves out of the way so the message of the Word is paramount.

But just as other things intended to be blessings can be misused, so can the power of high-impact communication. History is proof of that—even recent history. Charlatans, unscrupulous men, and liars have long mastered these principles and used them for their own gain. Nothing of lasting and eternal value can be done without the gracious power of the Holy Spirit, but, also, a great deal of harm and confusion can result if such powerful principles are abused.

How can we know that we use these precepts to a good end? What separates sanctified communication from indifferent speech? What safeguards can we take that will keep our motives pure and our purpose true?

THE INTEGRITY OF THE HEART

What keeps our message pure is the purity of a heart cleansed and kept by Jesus Christ. That is what separates our communication from every other

147

kind in the world. It has been so often repeated that it has become cliché, but the heart of the matter is the matter of the heart. Too many communicators try to reach the heart by way of the mind, but their approach is backward. Great leaders have always known that they had to reach the hearts of their followers. The teachers who make a lifelong impact are those who grip the hearts of their students. Great communicators like Augustine, Jonathan Edwards, and Charles Spurgeon wrote extensively on touching hearts, but they were in good company. Jesus himself focused on a ministry of the heart, one that flowed from his heart to the hearts of his listeners.

Who are the great leaders and world-changers that come to your mind? They possibly include people like:
- Anne Sullivan, Helen Keller's teacher
- General William Booth, founder of the Salvation Army
- Mother Teresa, servant to the masses of India
- Mahatma Gandhi, liberator of India
- Martin Luther King, civil rights leader
- Lech Walesa, opponent of communism and former president of Poland
- Billy Graham, Baptist evangelist and preacher to presidents

And what do they have in common? They are not equally educated or talented. No, their secret was that they knew how to grab the hearts of people. After that, changing the world just happens.

Why do you think people listened when Jesus stood and spoke? It was not his good looks, because Isaiah prophesied that "He had no beauty or majesty to attract us to him, nothing in his appearance that we should desire him" (Isa. 53:2b). People did not stop and listen to Jesus because he had great training and academic credentials, for he was just a Nazarene carpenter. They wanted to listen to him because in his very manner he communicated his heart to them, and they responded.

Jesus himself said as much in Matthew 11:29. Notice the only credential Jesus offered was not his mind but his heart: "Take my yoke upon you and learn from me, for I am gentle and humble in heart, and you will find rest for your souls." Of course, the mind is important, but in communication, as in loving God, the heart comes first. In Matthew 22:37 Jesus replied, ""Love the Lord your God with all your heart and with all your soul and with all your mind."" We don't think the order of his words is arbitrary. The heart comes first.

Who are the people in your life who have gripped your heart? What teachers, mentors, leaders, or pastors have really had an impact? List some of them here.

_____

_____

_____

_____

_____

The people you have listed probably are a very diverse bunch with different outlooks, backgrounds, educational levels, and professions. But they all share one thing: they reached your heart.

Now for the real question: Whose list do *you* want to make?

GOD VALUES HEARTS

In the Old Testament alone you will find mention of the heart 621 times. In the New Testament, "heart(s)" occurs 163 times. In the four Gospels alone, you can see the prominence of the heart because the evangelists use it some 55 times. The inference is easy to make: God cares about hearts. But more than just how often the word is used, one can discover the importance of the heart by *what* God says.

In God's book of wisdom, he advises us, "Above all else, guard your heart, for it is the wellspring of life" (Prov. 4:23). In other words, the heart is at the very center of life. And that valuable heart is to be treasured, guarded, and nurtured. Solomon told his son, "My son, give me your heart and let your eyes keep to my ways" (Prov. 23:26). This verse links the eyes—the power of the visual—with the centrality of the heart. What a powerful combination! God was telling us that we always move toward whatever we focus on, so if we keep our eyes focused on his ways, it is easier to keep our heart centered on him.

Further explaining this concept, Jesus said, "'For where your treasure is, there your heart will be also'" (Luke 12:34). Too often our values are not reflected in what we say they are, but in where our heart is and what our heart desires, and are revealed by how we spend our time and our money. In other words, it is impossible to hide the content of our heart over the course of time. Try hard as we might, the heart will bubble out in our behavior.

It is not the literal heart that we are talking about or that God was talking about. It is not that purely physical heart that God gave us to power our physical body. No, the heart that God refers to is the heart of our passion and emotional energy. It can best be conceived as that spiritual and emotional heart that takes residence in the feeling brain. This is the power plant—the heart that powers our will, our emotions, and our passion. And this heart, similar to all powerful things, can be used for good or for ill. It is our job to use it for good, and there is a way.

For a heart that honors God means more than just behavior. Many people have the ability to fake it. Still others develop a form of religion that is a habit but not a reality. Jesus warned about just going through the motions when he indicted his own generation by saying, "These people honor me with their lips, but their hearts are far from me" (Matt. 15:8). It is not enough to just learn how to speak. We must learn how to be. Speaking with bold assurance means communicating like Jesus. Our heart and our words must be in sync. That is the real key.

We must heed Solomon's advice in Proverbs 22:17–18: "Pay attention and listen to the sayings of the wise; apply your heart to what I teach, for it is pleasing when you keep them in your heart and have all of them ready on your lips." If our heart is applied to wisdom, we will have the right words ready on our lips. This is one of the most difficult concepts for most people to understand because our educational system and society teaches us that the rational facts are everything. All we have to do is know the facts and figures and communicate the data, and people will get them. What people get, however, is our hearts.

Melody was a leading professional fund-raiser for a charity she believed in. Not only did she encourage others to support her company, but she was a regular donor herself, until she discovered that the charity had begun supporting causes that conflicted with her Christian conscience and belief.

Though she quit donating her own money, she reasoned that she was a professional and that she should continue doing her job. She was good enough that she could still connect with potential donors and *act* as if she believed in the charity even though she did not.

But inside she felt empty. Finally, Melody decided to make a major life change. She took a job with a smaller company and for a smaller salary, but she believed in what she was doing. She placed a higher priority on her ease of conscience and peace of mind, and she could do her job with conviction and commitment!

To communicate effectively, we have to speak to the hearts and minds of our audience or our listeners, whether it be one person or a thousand people. But you never will get to a person's mind without getting to his heart first. God values hearts, and so should we.

HEART PRINCIPLES WORK

Most of the self-help and positive-thinking books that crowd bookstores and libraries have some faith principles that will indeed work, but they will soon pass away. Consequently, our culture sees temporal results to temporal faith, and so believes that temporal faith is all that is necessary. Many people are content to have the shadow of truth rather than the reality and eternity that Christ alone offers.

By the same token, the heart principles of communication work for anyone, yet they can only achieve results based on the content of the heart from which the communication comes. In other words, if *anyone* learns to communicate well, she can rouse passion and elicit a certain response from her audience. But the Bible is clear about the heart of an unbeliever: it is deceitful and desperately wicked. No one can even comprehend it (Jer. 17:9). Because people have good intentions, they assume that their actions are proper. The ones they lead follow them because they believe the same.

People who are passionate about the environment, human rights, politics, and business can speak well and inspire listeners to action. Throughout history even evil dictators, unprincipled politicians, and dangerous hate-mongers have reaped the results of their passion and misguided conviction. Some, even in the Christian world, have learned to mimic desirable behaviors and appear sincere. To the degree that they are passionate and persuasive, and use the nine communication skills well, they can experience a degree of success in their field.

Yet there is a huge difference between that kind of accomplishment and the impact that a Christian communicator desires. Other speakers can have passion, but their passion is limited to the temporal. If they have good intentions and a worthy cause, yet they do not share Christ, the best they can accomplish is to make the world a better place to go to hell from. If a Christian merely learns to manipulate his delivery style without allowing the Holy Spirit to change his character, he stands in danger of God's judgment.

The Christian heart is different. We have been given a new heart, a clean heart. And that heart is the wellspring of our passion and conviction. It is the power source of the emotional connection that we must make with our listeners. And that connection can be made in behavior, and just as importantly, it can be made in our content!

CHAPTER 27
Speaking to the Heart

Jesus was a master communicator because he not only spoke from his own heart, but he also directed his speech to the hearts of others. He changed minds by touching hearts. More than anyone else, Jesus demonstrated that the way to connect with people was to give them more than just information. The key is to give them yourself.

THE JESUS METHOD

Jesus certainly taught a lot of information. The entire Bible hinges on his life and teaching. The Old Testament would make no sense without it. Paul would have no teaching were it not for Jesus. We intensely study what Jesus said so that we may know God's will. But isn't it ironic that Jesus' teaching was so simple. He never gave a lecture on evangelism, but he told the parables of the lost sheep, the lost coin, and the lost son (Luke 15). When questioned about the extent of the law and defining who our neighbor is, he responded with the heart-tugging story of the Good Samaritan.

Jesus never trivialized his answers with sentimentality, but he never confused or alienated his audience with doctrine and details either. Jesus demonstrated that no one has to make a choice between information and emotion. He exemplified the perfect interplay between the two.

Even today his stories and parables have emotional impact. Only the most hardened reader could peruse the story of the rich man and Lazarus and not feel the terror of a man in hell, crying and begging for someone to warn his living brothers of the judgment to come. At the conclusion of the Sermon on the Mount, the greatest sermon ever preached, Jesus summed it all up with a story, the tale of the wise man and the foolish man. After laying the highest ethical standards the world had ever heard, Jesus closed with a stark emotional picture of the calm and stalwart assurance of the person who obeys him and the complete calamity of the one who hears but disregards his teaching.

Over and over again, Jesus tugged at the hearts of his audience. Sometimes his words startle and shock, but they nevertheless connect on an emotional level, not primarily a cerebral one. Imagine being with him when a Gentile woman comes and asks for a miracle. Contrary to anything we might expect, Jesus answers, "'. . . for it is not right to take the children's bread and toss it to their dogs'" (Mark 7:27). Yet Jesus knew exactly what he was doing. In being so raw and apparently abrasive, he was demonstrating the faith of the woman and her correct comprehension that she was not worthy of God's grace. Then he used the incident to teach a lesson about faith. It was one of the first times that Jesus' mission to the Gentiles was revealed. Had he merely granted the request, the scene and the lesson would not have been nearly as memorable.

CONNECTION, NOT EMOTIONALISM

Jesus never resorted to emotionalism—making mere emotion the goal. But he certainly wasn't afraid of using the emotions as a vehicle for his truth. Some communicators are content to tell a heartrending story that really has nothing to do with the point they are trying to make. They mistakenly think that if they can just get an audience to cry or laugh or sympathize, then they have done their job. Jesus certainly touched emotions, but it was always appropriate and fitting to his subject matter and to his listeners.

Others fall short on the opposite extreme. The ones who fail to communicate on an emotional level have the best of intentions. They usually believe that all they need do is to communicate the information, deliver the data, and the Holy Spirit will energize and apply the truth of the Word no matter how poorly they deliver it. Some even excuse their own laziness and lack of preparation in this way.

No one would argue that the Holy Spirit can and sometimes does use the Word of God even when it is poorly delivered. We could all cite stories and individuals whose testimonies bear witness to this. But the issue is not what the Holy Spirit *can* do, but what he *usually* does and what pleases him. Frankly, we are presumptuous to give him less than our best. We fail miserably when we communicate the most exciting and liberating message in the world with anything less than passion and excellence.

History bears witness to God's use of those who are willing to surrender all of their time and energy to his use. God did not use Chrysostom, Augustine, Luther, Calvin, Whitefield, Wesley, Spurgeon, Moody, or Graham because of their eloquence or passion, but they became passionate and eloquent because of their conviction about their message. And God used them.

Jesus spoke to hearts and changed minds, and that is still the most effective way of communicating God's truth today. Our message should be filled with images, with emotional impact, with stories and parables that highlight and drive home the content of our message.

Hershael:

Early in my ministry at the Ashland Avenue Baptist Church, I was preaching Colossians 2 and 3, the great text in which Paul explains that you cannot be holy by keeping the law, but that holiness comes from focusing on Christ and heavenly things. He goes on to explain that the "old man," that person that existed before we trusted Christ, is actually dead, but that we must go on to put to death the things that are related to the old man—his deeds and desires—and that we must clothe ourselves in the things that belong to the "new man." I wanted to illustrate that God has clothed us in the righteousness of Christ and that our deeds must match it like a pair of shoes should match a suit or a dress.

I related that my wife, Tanya, had gotten tired of an old, worn-out, dilapidated pair of Topsiders I had that made my feet feel wonderful, but they looked disgusting! Months after I thought she had thrown them away, I was getting ready to preach one Sunday morning and was rummaging in my closet looking for something when I was delighted to find my favorite pair of shoes. I was elated! It was like running into an old friend. I already had on my suit pants and shirt, but I had to run out to the car for something, so I just stepped into those old ugly shoes. I felt as though I was stepping into warm water when I put those shoes on.

Later that morning as I was preaching, just as I was making a dramatic point, my eyes fell to my feet and, to my horror, I realized that I was still wearing those shoes. Right in the pulpit, in front of hundreds of people, and with a nice suit, I was wearing ugly, frayed, and frazzled shoes because I had forgotten that I was wearing them. To say the least, I was terribly embarrassed.

Then I made my point. "Have you ever been rummaging in the store of memories that have been hiding in the corner of your mind? Suddenly, you discover the memory of a sin long past, long ago forsaken, but instead of repulsion it brings delight to your mind. You remember it fondly rather than in shame. You think of it as pleasurable, and before you know it, you have fallen into it again. You are still a child of God, still clothed in the righteousness of God, but you have slipped into the comfort of past sin, and it doesn't go with what you are wearing now. It belongs to the old man."

For such a simple illustration, drawn from my everyday life, it had a profound impact. For years following that sermon, struggling church members would frequently come into my office, hang their heads, and softly say, "Pastor, I slipped into an old pair of shoes this week." Immediately I knew what they meant. The power of a simple image had helped them recognize and deal with sin in their lives in a way that mere information probably would not have done.

SHARP PRINCIPLES

You can use the same principles that Jesus used to get to a person's heart. You can employ five methods to help you make the emotional connection that Jesus demonstrated. Together the five techniques form the acronym SHARP, and they serve to hone your message to pierce the armor of resistance and boredom that listeners often wear. By punctuating your message with these five methods, you make your audience want to hear you and pay attention to your content. You give listeners a handle for understanding and remembering your content.

<u>S</u>HARP—The Story

The first technique is to tell a story. Including a story that is interesting, engaging, entertaining, relevant to listeners' lives, and related to your point is one of the most effective ways to generate and hold listeners' interest. It is one thing to tell a person that Jesus can save them, but it is much more effective to tell them how he saved *you*. Anyone can tell a person whose marriage is in trouble that God *can* deliver them, but the listener will be much more encouraged if you can tell a story of when and how he restored someone's marriage when she was in trouble too. The story helps the listener identify with the truth and also to remember it in a context.

Jesus loved to tell stories because the simplest people could understand them. They remembered them, too, because they were preserved in an early oral tradition until they were written down by the evangelists as they were inspired by the Holy Spirit.

One of the greatest mistakes you can make with a story, however, is to tell one that is irrelevant to your audience. Many books of "illustrations" are full of stories of dead Englishmen and forgotten figures of history. Your audience probably doesn't care about Napoleon, the painting of the Sistine Chapel, or Alexander the Great. You will be amazed to discover, however, that people are most interested in your personal stories. They enjoy hearing about your struggles, victories, and thoughts. Be careful, however, that you are never inappropriate by being too personal, too revealing—that you do not betray the confidences and privacy of the others in your life. Be especially sensitive to your family.

When Jesus told stories, he used images and parables that evoked familiar settings. He told the kind of tales that his listeners recognized and identified with. Be sure that your stories are related to your listeners' lives. You can use the occasional stories about ancient conquerors and personalities, but mix them in with more contemporary and relevant anecdotes.

S<u>H</u>ARP—*Humor*

Nothing predisposes people to like you and listen to you like a good sense of humor. The ability to take a lighthearted look at oneself or surrounding events is one of the secrets of great communicators. Humor creates a special bond between you and your listeners. It's virtually impossible to dislike someone who makes us laugh, who helps us enjoy ourselves. A sense of humor—whether sharp and explosive or dry and witty—makes you appear more genial, warm, and likeable. The strong, pleasurable emotions people associate with good fun and high spirits make your message enjoyable to listen to—and memorable.

Our feeling brains use strong emotions—including the emotions that trigger smiles and laughter—to saturate our conscious brains with vivid impressions that result in greater retention of the message.

Humor is different, though, from telling jokes. Our advice is don't tell jokes. Leave the jokes to comedians. Too often communicators try to be funny by telling jokes and they flop for numerous reasons. The slightest variation in timing can ruin a joke. A misplaced word can destroy a punch line. Telling a joke that everyone knows just makes you look silly. Jokes are not the best way to be humorous, but the ability to take a lighthearted look at yourself, at the world around you, or at the human condition can really open an audience to you.

Hershael:
Evangelist David Miller, my friend from Arkansas who is confined to a wheelchair, has a wonderful icebreaker. For years he was able to stand to preach, but only after his personal attendant, Bill Williams, went through a very strange-looking

ritual of pulling David headlong out of his wheelchair and then straightening him up. The whole process usually took thirty to forty seconds and made the entire congregation gasp in disbelief and not a little fear. The tension and awkwardness were palpable. Then David, in his slow Arkansas drawl, would say, "Bill Williams has a lot of pull with me!" The audience would break up! The tension was gone, and listeners were in tune with him from then on!

Remember that comedy is not your goal, but _connection_ is. You just want to put your listeners at ease. Find your natural sense of humor and put it to use.

SH*A*RP—_Analogies_

A powerful way to make your speech memorable and picturesque is to use analogies as Jesus did. Jesus used earthy stories to describe heavenly truths. What is the kingdom of heaven like? It is like a man sowing, a pearl of great price, a mustard seed. A rich man getting into heaven is like a camel going through the eye of a needle. Jesus is the Shepherd, the Door, the Bread, the Water.

Whenever Jesus used an analogy, he fixed an image in the minds of his audience. Analogies are like hinges on which the doors of our minds swing. (There's an example of one, right there!)

Analogies provide a simple eloquence that can help speakers express themselves powerfully and at the same time can help listeners comprehend and grasp meaning. An analogy is a one-line illustration, a porthole of light illuminating your message and pegging it to your listener's memory.

SHA*R*P—_References_

If you want to help your listeners hear and accept your message, learn to use references effectively. References can either appeal to commonly accepted knowledge, reminding an audience of generally accepted facts, or they can lend support to your point of view by appealing to authority or the wisdom of others.

Jesus frequently referred to the Old Testament because it is God's inspired Word, recognized as such by the Jews, and the revelation of God's will. His ministry was saturated with Old Testament references used as an appeal to authority. Jesus often exposed the erroneous thinking of his contemporaries by citing the Old Testament. This lent support and authority to his message. When the Sadducees criticized his preaching about the Resurrection, Jesus quoted the familiar Old Testament declaration that Yahweh is the God of Abraham, Isaac, and Jacob, and that as such he is the God of the living, not of the dead.

Jesus also used references to establish commonly accepted views that needed correction too. In the Sermon on the Mount (in Matthew 5–7), for instance, Jesus followed the formula, "You have heard it said . . . but I say unto you . . ." In this way Jesus was reminding them of some beliefs that needed correction.

Your purpose in using references is not to impress, but to impact. Don't weigh down your presentation, but a sparing use of appropriate quotations, poems, references to common cultural or current events can help turn on the lights for an audience.

SHAR**P**—*Pictures*

In addition to making your own presence as interesting as possible, give your listeners something visual to look at whenever appropriate. Make your communication memorable with the use of bold, striking graphic aids, props, overheads, flip charts, or other sensory enhancements.

Pastors, professors, and teachers are increasingly finding the benefit of using PowerPoint presentations as they speak. Coupled with a fill-in-the-blank outline, sermon and lesson outlines flashed on a screen behind an active speaker are a powerful combination.

For added impact, mix assorted kinds of media (for example, use both overheads and video clips) in order to keep the visual dimension varied and interesting. Rehearse the visual part of your presentation so that transitions will be fluid rather than fumbling. Involve your listeners with your visuals; for example, ask questions of your audience and briefly tabulate their answers on an overhead transparency.

If you are teaching your class how to greet guests, for instance, write a script and rehearse a scenario with some willing class members. Anything you do to help your audience visually picture the truth you are teaching is a great help. When Jesus told his followers that they had to become like a child to enter heaven, he first took a little child in his lap. As they saw the simple adoration and obedience of that child, Jesus' words had a stronger impact because they were visual.

The content of our message is crucial, but we must follow Jesus' pattern to make sure that our content first reaches the heart. By using the SHARP principles to gain and maintain our listeners' interest, we can have greater impact and lasting effect—just like Jesus.

CHAPTER 28
The Truth of Presenting Yourself

Great communicators share a passion for constant improvement. They understand that they never arrive at a plateau of ultimate communication skills. Instead, they become lifelong students of their culture, themselves, and their techniques of reaching others. The principles of bold assurance do not provide anyone with a way to become a perfect communicator, but they provide a surefire method of steady improvement over the course of a lifetime. Reading this book—or any other book—won't make you an instant success. But if you consistently *apply* these principles, you will move to the next level, then the next level, and the next.

Like speaking, the price of excellence is transparency and vulnerability. People will listen to your message because they see your own passion and confidence in what you are saying. The more vulnerable you are to them, the more credible they find you and, therefore, the more they pay attention to what you are saying. But you must exhibit that same vulnerability and transparency as you prepare and strive to improve.

Feedback is the breakfast of champions. Great Olympic athletes thrive on coaching, watching themselves on video, getting advice from other athletes, and from the way their performance feels. In their perpetual struggle to exact their best performance from their efforts, they rely on many different techniques of evaluation.

Accepting criticism—even the best-intentioned and constructive criticism—is often painful. But if you really want to take your speaking to the next level of effectiveness and impact, you must identify the limiting factors—those habits and behaviors that hold you back—and get rid of them. Learning how to give and to receive feedback is an integral part of gaining bold assurance in your communication competence. You must be open to the suggestions of others, which develops your ability to think on the perceptual level, and you must learn to evaluate your own performance.

Thankfully, there are specific ways for you to obtain and appreciate the evaluations of others as well as to evaluate yourself. There are three basic kinds of feedback: people, audio, and video. Each of them has a great benefit and will serve you well. Once you know how to get and to give that kind of feedback, you have a ladder on which to climb to the next level, one rung at a time.

THE 3 X 3 RULE

Not all criticism is created equal. Criticism might range from carping, caviling, and censure that is anything but helpful, to ingratiating approbation and acclaim that is undeserved. In short, if you just

> *Oh wad some power the giftie gie us to see oursels as others see us!*
> ROBERT BURNS

ask for criticism, you cannot be certain that the criticism is well reasoned and helpful beyond the immediate situation or even beyond the opinion of that one person. Furthermore, you usually feel the need to filter what she says based on her predisposition to you. You are intuitively aware that your grandmother will probably give you a different evaluation of a performance than a communications expert.

So how can you get a person to give you an honest evaluation that is already filtered for you? How can you get the rival to affirm and encourage you when appropriate and your grandmother to tell you those areas where even *she* can see room for improvement?

The answer is a simple tool for people feedback called the 3 x 3 rule. Whenever you speak, ask someone who heard you to tell you three things that they thought were good and effective, and three areas where you have room for improvement. This simple method acknowledges that no speech, sermon, or talk is completely good or bad. We need to know the things we are doing that work so we can hone them and duplicate them, but we also need to know the things that we do that get in the way. We need balanced feedback.

The 3 x 3 rule is a powerful tool because it both affirms and challenges us. Just as the gauges on a car tell us both that the engine is running properly *and* that it needs servicing, so we need a gauge to remind us of the areas that deserve and require a greater investment of our time.

You can use the 3 x 3 rule every time you speak. Even when you think you were really "on" you need to know what specifically helped you deliver that content well. Don't be satisfied with compliments! If someone begins to compliment you and tell you how great you were, you can thank him appropriately and then say, "I like for people to tell me three things that they noticed and thought were good, and three things that I can improve. You have already told me one thing you like, so tell me two other things and then give me three areas you think I can improve."

The benefits of this simple technique are virtually limitless. As you open yourself up to this kind of constructive criticism, you show others that you really are transparent—it wasn't just an act when you spoke. It further makes the people you ask for advice think through your presentation once more, thus sealing it in their hearts and minds.

On a personal level, the 3 x 3 rule will keep you passionate for excellence and growth throughout life. You develop the habit of striving for quality in everything you do. And it will help you develop a thick skin too. You become more accustomed to hearing about the ways you need to improve, and it will change the way you respond to criticism, even when it's unjust.

Finally, the 3 x 3 rule makes you sensitive to helping others. You won't just dump negatives on someone, but you learn to look for the positives in everything and everyone around you. Imagine using the 3 x 3 rule when you offer criticism to your spouse, your teen, or your coworkers. Whether helping others achieve their best or improving yourself, few things help you like this rule.

Audio Feedback

An audio recording helps you hear yourself the way others hear you. If you are a computer user, you may have a microphone with your computer. Use it! Record yourself and play it back. How do you sound? What would you think if you heard a voice like that?

One way of learning to hear yourself the way others hear you is to voice mail yourself. If you work in a business with a voice-mail system, send a copy to your own voice mail so you can listen to the message. Pay attention to your voice. Does it command attention? Does your voice, like a roller coaster, rise and fall with inflection that conveys energy and passion? In short, will your message reach out to your recipient?

If you give a formal speech or presentation, make sure you get at least an audio recording. Even if there is no sound system or formal recording, you can invest a little in a microcassette recorder and carry it with you. If you find it impossible to unobtrusively place it on the lectern, have someone in the audience hold it or just place it on the table in front of him (since you won't really be stuck behind the lectern anyway!). You can listen to it later and evaluate yourself.

When listening to your own voice, ask yourself these questions:
- Do I get my listener's attention?
- How many fillers do I use?
- Do I repeat myself?
- Does my voice "smile"?

If an honest evaluation reveals a monotonous, passionless, or lifeless voice, then make the necessary changes. Infuse your voice with life by using inflection. And smile, even when no one can see you. No matter how silly it sounds or feels, your voice reflects the presence or absence of a smile. You cannot possibly sound happy if you don't put a smile on your face when you talk.

Using audio feedback makes you accustomed to hearing and evaluating your voice, the most adaptable tool in your communications toolbox. You develop a passion for excellence and growth while you strive to increase your ability to impact others.

VIDEO FEEDBACK

The greatest tool available to a speaker is his ability to actually see himself and notice every behavior and nuance of his performance. You may question the 3 x 3 feedback you get from an observer, thinking him too kind or too harsh. You may find it difficult to equate that funny-sounding voice on the tape with the one you hear in your head. But when you see the tape and hear the voice coming from the mouth that's the same one you see in the mirror, there can be no denying the truth, whether better or worse than you imagined.

After years of repairing scarred and disfigured faces, plastic surgeon Dr. Maxwell Maltz made an ironic discovery: no matter how successful his efforts and how complete the recovery, his patients did not automatically change their perception of themselves. They often still felt "ugly."

Once after Dr. Maltz had removed a hideous scar from the face of an otherwise beautiful eighteen-year-old girl, he was shocked to find that, even though he had restored her beauty and left her skin flawless, she told him that she could see no difference. Finally, when he could not convince her, he got a "before" picture and held it beside the mirror. "Now," he asked, "do you see the difference?" After a long pause, she softly answered, "Yes, doctor, I see that the scar is gone, but I don't *feel* any different."

Maxwell Maltz found that people with physical disfigurements undermine themselves. Thinking themselves somehow less than other people, they act that way, and the feeling becomes a self-perpetuating cycle. Day by day, this self-sabotaging behavior digs deeper and deeper grooves into their self-image. The more people see themselves as inadequate, the more they limit themselves. The more they limit themselves, the more others see them as inadequate. It's the cruelest of all vicious cycles.

And it's not just people with physical disfigurements who undermine and limit themselves. You know it and I know it: we are all in the same boat. You don't have to have a scar on your face or a misshapen limb to feel unattractive and inadequate. Some of us wear our scars on the inside, whether they were put there by someone else or whether they are self-inflicted.

And nothing can change our perception of ourselves like simply seeing the truth. Previous generations may have practiced in front of the mirror, but today's video technology puts power at your fingertips that no other generation has ever had! You can use it to see yourself as others see you— and that means you can use it to transform yourself. All we have to do is plug it in, turn it on, and zap! The power to radically transform our self-image and personal effectiveness lights up the nearest TV screen!

How can a video camera do all that? When we see our presentation played back on video, we become the audience. We have the same objective vantage point as the audience. We see ourselves as others see us.

Bert:

Maggie was a slender and personable lady of twenty-eight when I first met her. She was working as an administrative assistant to a busy executive. She was effective and confident and attractive. But she didn't know it.

I didn't know that she didn't know it until I ran into her at a meeting we were both attending. She had completed our two-day workshop that incorporates extensive video feedback. Whenever I get the chance, I always barrage new graduates with such questions as, "How did you like the seminar?" "What could we do better?" "What's different in your life?" "Are you using what you learned?" I asked Maggie all the usual questions. Her reply was succinct.

"I'm pretty."

That's all she said. But with that she said everything. I didn't need to ask Maggie the details. I knew what she meant. I knew the power of video feedback.

For the first time she saw herself in a different way. For the first time she saw herself as others really see her.

I later learned that, during her childhood, Maggie had been mercilessly teased by her older sisters for supposedly being skinny and unattractive. She grew up believing these cruel taunts were true. As competent and attractive as she was, she didn't know it. She didn't believe it—until she saw herself on videotape.

As you watch the video, you are able to see things of which you were not aware. There will certainly be some things that you want to eliminate, but most people are actually shocked to discover that the video reveals them as *better* than they thought previously. Video feedback not only helps us eliminate the limiting factors—unconscious twitches, nose scratches, and awkward postures—but, more often, it liberates us from the limits of our self-perception.

The Goal of Feedback

Learning how to use various forms of feedback provides us the tools to keep growing throughout our lives. We can move from one level of performance and knowledge to another. If our goal is to be as proficient as possible, we need to understand a little about how we learn.

For every skill there exists four stages of learning. The first stage is *unconscious incompetence.* Have you ever seen a two-year-old jump into a swimming pool for the first time? The child is not aware that he doesn't know how to swim—and so he sinks until someone rescues him. But that failure has an effect on him. Now, for the first time, he *knows* that he does not know. He has moved to the second stage, *conscious incompetence.* He loves the water, and it looks cool and inviting on a hot summer day, but his memory of what happened before keeps him on the deck and out of the water.

So his parents sign him up for swimming lessons. Now he has a coach who gives him a surefire method of learning to swim. He teaches him to count, as though to music, so he can make his strokes, his kicks, and his breathing regular and synchronized. An eager and motivated learner, the child painstakingly follows the teacher's instruction. "One stroke, two stroke, turn head, breathe! One stroke, two stroke, turn head, breathe!" Finally he knows *how* to swim, but he has to concentrate on it with every movement. He has reached the level of *conscious competence.*

Since he loves the water so much, the child visits the pool every day. Before long he no longer has to count or think about when it is time to breathe. His swimming is no longer labored, awkward, or dependent on his counting. Now he glides effortlessly through the water with the most natural motion imaginable. He has moved to *unconscious competence.* He acts out of an ingrained habit rather than a laborious effort.

Every time you learn something—*really* learn it—you move through these four stages, at least you do if you master it. Can you imagine driving if you had to consciously tell yourself, "Apply brakes now—not too hard—easy! Easy!" You couldn't have a conversation, turn on the radio, or even think of anything else while you drive. But if you are a good driver, you can act without having to stop and think about it.

Particularly in your communication ability, stage four is your goal, and you can get there. It just takes the combination of time, effort, and practice. You have to consciously choose those habits you want to form, and feedback helps you get there.

The Four Stages of Speaking

Speakers the world over fall into four basic levels of effectiveness. Each has different characteristics of emotion, behavior, attitude, and position. We all are in one of these four stages of speaking. What is important is to find out which one you are in, and move to the next level. We grow from stage 1 to stage 4 as we learn more about ourselves and our ability to control feeling-brain fear, and as we practice, and as we speak.

The stages are:

Stage 1: The Nonspeaker, characterized by:

Emotion: Terror. This person is virtually scared to death of standing up and speaking before a group. Even the prospect of stating his name and introducing himself before a group fills him with anxiety. Often the non-speaker is characterized by extreme shyness.

Behavior: Rarely Speaks. The nonspeaker stays away from any situation when he might be called on to speak.

Attitude: Avoidance. He is passive, with excuses. "Gee, I'd love to, but I don't feel well." "Oops, that's my pinochle night." "Sorry, got to take our iguana to the vet." Occasionally this person will get trapped into making a presentation at the office or teaching an occasional Sunday school class, but usually he is very adept at making excuses to avoid presenting himself publicly.

Position: Support. Usually he has a low skill level because he has little experience or ability as a communicator, so he works in a job that doesn't require communication skills but serves the church in a physical or financial way.

Stage 2: The Occasional Speaker

Emotion: Fear. Hers isn't paralyzing fear but is sufficiently serious to limit her effectiveness. It is this fear that keeps her from volunteering. On those occasions when she is cajoled (or conned) into speaking, her nervousness usually shows. (The majority of people are in this stage.)

Behavior: Speaks Occasionally. She can be coaxed into taking a speaking assignment, but she would rarely volunteer.

Attitude: Acceptance, with Reluctance. She has a growing awareness of the importance of being able to speak effectively. She probably knows she must be able to present her ideas in order to reach or bless others, but she may not know how to go about it.

Position: A Front-line Doer. She has growing ability. The occasional speaker is not locked into a pattern of hibernation and abject terror. She has tried public speaking, and she has survived. She learns that she can improve with work.

Stage 3: The Willing Speaker

Emotion: Tension. He has a trace of the old fight-or-flight response, but it's no longer a hindrance—more of an annoyance. Positive emotions pervade. This speaker has learned to anticipate rather than dread the speaking experience. He finds that extra edge of tension uncomfortable but stimulating, just like an athlete before a race. He knows he will do well, but he's coiled and tensed for the performance, not complacent.

Behavior: Speaks Often. He's vocal and articulate. He readily utters his mind in meetings and is not intimidated by the Bible study class he teaches.

Attitude: Willing. He experiences butterflies, but they fly in formation.

Position: Management. He may not think of himself as a "public speaker," but he has the skills to pull it off. And the confidence.

Stage 4: The Communicator

This person understands that speaking is part of his or her job description.

Emotion: Stimulation. He feels an excitement about speaking and is genuinely stimulated by speaking. He enjoys the feedback he gets from the audience, not to mention the applause or the encouragement afterwards.

Behavior: Speaks Always. He has embraced the art of turning the fight-or-flight reaction into positive energy. Adrenaline is his ally.

Attitude: Eagerness. He doesn't hesitate to present himself and his convictions. In fact, he jumps at the chance! He knows the rewards to be reaped and the impact he can have for Christ.

Position: Leadership. He is recognized as a person who attracts, persuades, and motivates people by the way he communicates. He inspires and commands.

Your growth as a speaker will depend largely on your desire to improve, but with the right tools of evaluation, introspection, and feedback your abilities will steadily and significantly improve. Getting feedback from others, from audio and video sources, and determining to constantly hone your skills will help you move from terror to fear to tension and ultimately to stimulation. As you learn to harness the nervous energy and transform it into a positive force, you rid yourself of the factors that limit your effectiveness and impact. The message of the gospel deserves such lifelong effort.

CHAPTER 29
Telling Your Story

Imagine that you are walking down a city street one day and you witness an automobile crash. Right before your eyes one car blindsides another vehicle. A few days later, you are subpoenaed and asked to appear in court as a witness. Before you testify, you sit in the courtroom and hear the testimony of other witnesses. The others are all expert witnesses. They talk about the direction and velocity of the cars. Others explain about the weight and stopping distances. Police testify about the measurement of the skid marks on the pavement.

Then comes your turn. You don't say a word about any of those things. All you do is tell what you saw. You don't judge stopping distances, car velocity, vehicle weight, value of the cars involved, or fault of the drivers. All you do is describe the one thing you know for sure: you saw what happened.

You may not know all about the Bible that you want to know. Perhaps you are a new believer or an immature believer. Maybe you lament that you need to study the Word of God more. Though you are certainly correct in your feeling, you must never let what you *don't* know keep you from telling what you *do* know. Let pastors and seminary professors be the expert witnesses. You can always tell what you have seen in your own life.

In other words, you must be ready and willing to tell what Jesus has done for *you*. You must be prepared to tell how you came to know Christ in a simple, passionate way. Whether you have thirty seconds or thirty minutes, you should know how to tell how God has worked in *your* life.

God gave *you* that story and no one else. No one can do it for you. No one can witness for you any more than she can believe in Christ for you. Your salvation was personal and so is your testimony, the story that God has given you. Tell it! It is the best and ideal place for you to begin to apply the principles of bold assurance that you have learned in this book. You cannot save or convince anyone, but you can tell your story in a persuasive, passionate, and personal manner. Whether she believes in your Christ or not, make certain that she knows *you* believe in your Christ.

Something sacred and wonderful occurs when you share your life with others for no other reason than your love for Christ and for them. Jesus shared his life through dying, so we must share ours through living.

REAP THE HARVEST

Reaping a harvest of souls is much like a farmer reaping a harvest of grain. Proverbs 14:4 says, "Where there are no oxen, the manger is empty, but from the strength of an ox comes an abundant harvest." When we are strong and able and willing to share ourselves and our stories, there will be an abundant harvest, but when we are withdrawn, shy, bashful, and inhibited, the manger will be empty. And as we know, the harvest is plentiful, but there are few to reap the harvest. Will you be one of those who will reap the harvest?

Jesus was always looking for the harvest. When he was at the well talking to the Samaritan woman, it was because of his actions and words that she told many others. John 4:41 says, "And because of his words many more became believers."

All around us are unique opportunities to share ourselves, if we are open to them. Jesus was talking to us also when he said to his disciples in Mark 13:9, "'You must be on your guard. You will be handed over to the local councils and flogged in the synagogues. On account of me you will stand before governors and kings as witnesses to them.'" The same warnings and promises attend us nearly two thousand years later.

Remember Proverbs 15:7: "The lips of the wise spread knowledge; not so the hearts of fools." And 1 Peter 3:15: "But in your hearts set apart Christ as Lord. Always be prepared to give an answer to everyone who asks you to give the reason for the hope that you have. But do this with gentleness and respect." Peter was careful to tell us that the content of the reason for our hope is not sufficient. We must have the right manner as well. What a picture of love we paint when we give the reason for our hope in gentleness and respect!

BE PROACTIVE

Always keep in mind what the wise James said in his book in 1:22: "Do not merely listen to the word, and so deceive yourselves. Do what it says." If you just read the principles of this book or any book, but don't apply them, you have gained nothing. How much more true is that of reading the Word of God!

Have you ever read through Proverbs and been struck by the number of verses that talk about "the sluggard"? God is telling us that we cannot ooze into the kingdom of God, but choose into it, to be proactive, to take action, to have that forward lean.

And if we do not take action, we don't hurt just ourselves. Others are affected as well—perhaps for eternity. "One who is slack in his work is brother to one who destroys" (Prov. 18:9). If we don't tell our story, we aren't much better than someone who tries to discredit and damage the gospel. Silence is an expensive, wasteful disobedience.

Hard work is expected of God's servants, and if we don't take it that way, we will suffer for it. Proverbs 6:10–11 warns, "A little sleep, a little slumber, a little folding of the hands to rest—and poverty will come on you like a bandit and scarcity like an armed man."

Many verses urge us to diligence and hard work throughout the Bible, but one of the most poetic is found in Proverbs 24:30–34.

> I went past the field of the sluggard, past the vineyard of the man who lacks judgment; thorns had come up everywhere, the ground was covered with weeds, and the stone wall was in ruins. I applied my heart to what I observed and learned a lesson from what I saw: A little sleep, a little slumber, a little folding of the hands to rest— and poverty will come on you like a bandit and scarcity like an armed man.

These are some of the same words that we saw earlier in Proverbs 6:11. If it was important enough for the Holy Spirit to include twice, we had best heed his words. We are to be vigilant and proactive, or else we will come to great ruin. We are to live life and to communicate our life with a forward lean.

THE BLESSING OF OBEDIENCE

Think of what a blessing you can be to others when you can share yourself and encourage them with a bold heart. Feeling the passion of conviction, transforming any nervousness into excitement and energy, you make that important emotional connection that makes them listen to what you are saying so the Word and the Holy Spirit are free to work. Remember Proverbs 12:25, "An anxious heart weighs a man down, but a kind word cheers him up."

When we encourage others, we spread love. We do the second of the greatest commandments. And we can experience more joy and spread hope. We can be encouragers to so many who have lost hope, who do not have faith. What better way to overcome our hesitancy than with the boldness that comes from realizing what the gospel can do in their lives?

"Consequently, faith comes from hearing the message, and the message is heard through the word of Christ" (Rom. 10:17). There is one great requirement for the Word to be heard: it has to be spoken. And it is best conveyed through each one of us to those who know us and trust us. God brought us into their lives for this very purpose.

Your words may fall on deaf ears, or ears not yet ready to hear, but your words will not come back void. The only way to fail is to never share your story with those you love. So be proactive, be a light in your world, and be salt in a tasteless environment—for that salt is sorely needed.

CHAPTER 30
Leading . . . and Beyond

The ability to communicate in large measure determines your ability to lead. Bill Hybels, founder of Willow Creek and an expert in communications, looks for leaders who are "100-watt bulbs." They speak out. And as John Maxwell says, leadership is influence, so everyone is in some way a leader because everyone influences *someone*. What we need to consider is that God wants all of us to be leaders, at least in that way, for he has commanded us. But there is much more than that in store for those with a forward lean.

When you effectively communicate your faith, you are leading someone to Christ. When you teach a lesson, you are leading your class to adapt and apply the principles of the passage you present. When you give a speech, you are leading your audience to buy into your ideas. When you are running a meeting, you are leading a group toward a goal. In all your communicating situations, you are leading by communicating—effectively.

As you apply the principles of bold assurance in your home, work, and personal ministry, you begin to realize your potential and the power to lead and mold the people around you. To use this God-given power to its fullest potential, a few principles will help develop your leadership skills.

LAWS FOR LEADERS

Leaders have character

Bold assurance is about having integrity. The word *integrity* literally means "united" or "single." Effective communication means walking with God in purity and being free of guile and deceit. If you are going to really lead others, you cannot be duplicitous. You cannot say one thing and do another.

To the contrary, being a powerful communicator means making your walk and your talk equal. Doing and saying the right thing with conviction and purpose breeds bold assurance and impacts others.

Sometimes we say, "Just be yourself," but that advice only works when your relationship with God results in godly character that shines in your behavior. To exercise the greatest leadership you must exhibit the greatest character. You must have integrity that translates into your words and inspires those around you to listen to your message. Leaders set the example.

Leaders cannot afford to be sarcastic

Sarcasm is humor that gets a cheap laugh, often used as a cover-up of something deeper. Of all forms of humor, sarcasm is the most demeaning and insulting to those against whom it is directed. Leaders encourage others and help them grow. Sarcasm grows no one. It only tears down and confuses others. And undermines trust in the leader!

> *Like a madman shooting firebrands or deadly arrows is a man who deceives his neighbor and says, "I was only joking!"*
> PROVERBS 26:18–19

Have you ever seen a leader who uses sarcasm to get laughter. Not very often, because it doesn't work for leaders. We all know people who are continuously kidding, needling, and using other forms of sarcasm, and whenever they talk, we can never be sure whether they mean what they say or are just kidding.

How can you believe and trust a leader if you're not sure that he means what he says? With sarcasm, we can never be sure. The words of a leader must always be credible; we must know that the person always means what he says. (We don't necessarily have to agree, of course.)

Say what you mean, but speak the truth in love. Sarcasm always communicates condescension and arrogance and has no place in the life of a leader.

Leaders focus on others

Just as Jesus did not come to be served but to serve, so great communicators focus on others. That is why we spend so much time learning to communicate in a way that removes distractions and opens channels of receptivity.

Leaders are never isolated

They realize that you cannot have impact on people at arm's length. You must get involved. Jesus called twelve disciples and invited them into his life. He wanted them to be *with* him. You cannot be a leader in isolation. You will have to be with people, maintain your integrity and passion, and share the message that God has given you. Shaping and leading others takes time as well as the proper message. Time is your most valuable personal currency, and you must spend it to reach others.

> The horse is made ready for the day of battle, but victory rests with the LORD.
> PROVERBS 21:31

THE TOUCH OF TEACHING

Speaking with bold assurance will give you impact, but it must begin with the responsibilities that God has given you right where you are. If you have a family, begin there. Use these principles in the way you teach your children, address your spouse, or talk with the family or guests at the dinner table.

As you apply these communication principles in everyday life, you will experience their power. At the heart of many domestic problems is an inability to talk and understand one another. As you monitor the subtle behaviors that send the wrong signals to your spouse or teen, you can change and become a greater encourager. Even when you have the unpleasant task of correcting your child's behavior, you can discipline in an encouraging and positive manner. If you learn to open a child's feeling brain so he can hear what you're saying, you will have more than just authority over your child. You will have *influence*.

Then broaden your circle of influence beyond your home to others. In your business, ministry, or professional life, strive to teach. Have you always harbored the desire to teach a Sunday school class, but been afraid to try it? Perhaps you have even tried, but with poor results. In the past you might have worked very hard to bring your class the right information, but you never realized that you were tranquilizing your listeners with your manner. Now is the time to change that! Visualize what can happen to that class if you energize and enliven your presentation with an enthusiastic presentation that is listener-centered and Bible-based!

The Power of Preaching

No one has a greater opportunity to impact others on a regular basis than preachers and pastors do. Unfortunately, too many preachers are just biblical data dumps, carefully interpreting the Bible but not reaching their audiences. By applying the principles presented in this book, a preacher can get a congregation to hear and reap the benefit of his study and preparation. What a waste it would be to spend so many years in education and seminary, study and preparation, only to bore a congregation! What a sin it is to make the most exciting book in the world a drudgery!

Preaching with power is an honored gift of God, and one that can best use the skills and approach of bold assurance. It is such an important and large subject that we plan to publish *Preaching with Bold Assurance,* a book specifically written for preachers. This book will combine an effective method of study and exegesis with a dynamic and appropriate guide to delivery.

At the heart of that book will be the principles that you have read here. When these concepts are applied and empowered with the Holy Spirit, sermon preparation can be much more productive and delivery can be much more effective. Combining the powerful truth of God's Word with the passionate presentation of God's servant is the way the Holy Spirit usually works. Though God can use *anything,* he usually uses those who are most available to him. And those who are most prepared.

Learn by Doing

There is no substitute for practice. If you wish to become an effective communicator, then look for opportunities to put these principles to work. In your family life, in your business or professional life, and in your ministry life. Find someone for whom you have a burden and share the gospel with her. Ask to be a substitute Bible study teacher or even start a class. Try preparing your lesson or sermon using the Decker Grid System instead of a manuscript.

We are held responsible for what we learn. You have moved to a level of conscious knowledge with the principles of this book. By incorporating them into your daily life and ministry, you will eventually move to unconscious knowledge as they become second nature to you. And the truth of

God's Word conveyed by the conduit of your integrity and delivery brings you a wonderful possession—bold assurance.

CHAPTER 31

Facing the Future with Bold Assurance

Myrna

"I never turn down an opportunity to speak now," Myrna says eagerly. A marriage and family therapist in her middle fifties, she had frequently been asked to speak about her area of expertise, but she always felt uncomfortable when she would relent and agree to speak. "Previously I shied away from some invitations, but now I have that *forward lean* and I have learned to actually enjoy risk taking. Since I learned the principles of bold assurance, I have had so many areas of growth in my life."

God had given Myrna wisdom and a desire to serve him through her practice, her church, and her family, but when it came to channeling that knowledge and her gifts into a format that others could understand and use, she often felt inadequate. She just wasn't sure that she was connecting when she spoke.

Now, after learning the same principles that you have just learned, Myrna's life has changed. She helps teach an adult Bible study in her church. A frequent host of workshops and seminars, she feels a connection with her audience when she speaks.

"One of the best things is that I have learned so much about the practical skills of preparation," Myrna says. "I used to overprepare so much, gathering far more material than was possible to use, yet I tried to fit it in anyway. Now I have cut my preparation time way down, and I'm more focused and realistic about time. Those little Post-it Notes guide me and keep me right on track."

Myrna finds that bold assurance principles help her sound much more confident and professional in little ways that make a big difference. Whenever she leaves a voice-mail message, she makes certain that it is clear and concise, rather than rambling and redundant.

And Myrna's skills are even blessing people who may never hear her speak. She and her husband, Jack, volunteer and represent a mission organization that ministers to untouchables in India. They realize that when they speak to a congregation or a missions committee, they can't overwhelm their listeners with facts. Instead, their goal is to make that emotional connection so that their audience actually *feels* the burden that they feel. A lot of Christians might make similar efforts, but Myrna and Jack have learned to make their effort *effective*.

JACK

"I never was afraid to make a presentation, but I always knew that I wasn't doing a very good job," Jack says. Even though he was successful in business and owned his own company, Jack realized that he wasn't living up to the standard that the Lord deserved. "I believe that Christians need to be excellent in *whatever* they do, and some of us are just an embarrassment. Bold assurance has helped me strive for excellence in a way that I did not before."

Like Myrna, Jack never turns down an opportunity to speak if his schedule is clear. He is a featured speaker now at retreats, in his church and denomination, and even in more difficult circumstances. "Recently I was asked to speak at the memorial service for a friend who had passed away." Knowing there would be many nonbelievers there, Jack relied on the Decker method and prepared a eulogy that comforted his audience. "It was difficult, but I stayed focused. I felt like I really helped and comforted them. I attribute it to the Decker method and my Post-it notes!"

Jack has noticed that bold assurance truths have especially helped him in his one-on-one relationships and encounters. "Now I always look for opportunities to share about Christ. I have a group of friends that I meet with, and we encourage one another and are doing a book study together. Two of the five are unconverted, and I am able to speak and share with them much more confidently and effectively than ever before."

As Jack contemplates the second half of his working life, he is intent on using his gifts and resources for the Lord. What he has learned from bold assurance has focused him and given him a method for effective service.

ERIKA

Erika, a bright and devoted young assistant in an investment banking firm, testifies that bold assurance has had the greatest impact on her personal life. "I first heard about it from a friend whose life had been changed dramatically through bold assurance. When I first began to study it, I thought, 'This is not for me. I am out of place.' But then I realized that this is about *serving the Lord* and it is for every believer—even me."

Though she is not often called on to make formal presentations, she says, "Bold assurance has helped me primarily in relationships with my family, friends, and even in my dating life. It is about kingdom building. It opens the doors of a friend's heart so I am able to speak to her from my heart. I am not intimidated anymore. I feel the courage to just share from my heart. In my dating life, too, I am able to speak to a date about spiritual things. I am able to open up, and God comes into that relationship in a more profound way."

Would she accept formal speaking opportunities if they came along? "Absolutely," she says. "I wouldn't feel out on a limb at all. One of the principles that bold assurance has taught me is that the righteous are as bold as a lion. We do not need to fear."

Now Erika devotes much of her time to being a coleader in small group studies of the workbook *Communicating with Bold Assurance.* In fact, she is currently leading a group for the fifth time because she knows what an investment this is in the lives of others and what huge dividends it has paid in her own life. Erika has a passion to build the Lord's kingdom through what she has learned.

YOU

There is nothing unique about Myrna, Jack, or Erika that enabled them to learn and to change. They do not possess any innate ability that you do not have. As a believer, you have the Word of God, the Spirit of God, and the command of God to take his message and to let it season your life and speech in every circumstance.

Take a moment and picture yourself a year from now, five years from now, a decade even, after learning and consistently applying the principles that you have learned. You are focused, directed, confident, and intentional in your witness and interaction with others. Other people enjoy talking to you and hearing you talk. They feel your heart when you communicate, and they like it. You have an impact on everyone around you because God's truth is constantly flowing through you.

God has given you a message that is unique to your life and experience. It is *your* story. Only you can tell it. Only you have been placed in the web of friends, associates, neighbors, and family who exist around you. Only you can reach them.

Now go do it—with Bold Assurance.

Further Resources

Contact Bold Assurance Ministries

Bold Assurance Ministries is a nonprofit organization that builds speaking confidence with God-given principles. The ministry provides information, training resources, and solutions to a broad array of communicating questions. To specifically help you apply the principles of this book, the ministry, together with LifeWay Christian Resources, has produced the video seminar *Communicating with Bold Assurance,* which is the recommended next step. (See information on page 184.)

Visit our Web site at www.boldassurance.com. Or contact us at:

Bold Assurance Ministries
P.O. Box 320189
San Francisco, CA 94132
(888) 988-2653

Contact the Authors

Bert Decker and Hershael York wrote this book to:
- Assure you that your communicating ability can be all that God intended.
- Provide skills and concepts that you can implement immediately.
- Point to solutions and tools you can use to further communicating effectiveness.
- Encourage followers of Christ to share their faith with others.

We would love to hear from you. Please E-mail us and tell us what you think of the ideas in this book. We would particularly appreciate 3 x 3 feedback. Please tell us what areas of interest that would be of further benefit to you. (We are currently working on *Preaching with Bold Assurance* and would like to apply further the principles of Bold Assurance to teaching and leading as well.)

Thank you for taking these ideas to heart. We look forward to hearing from you.

Communicating with Bold Assurance

Bert Decker's *Communicating with Bold Assurance*
VIDEO SEMINAR and the INTERACTIVE WORKBOOK will—

- Transform your fear of speaking into confidence.
- Identify and improve your communication skills.
- Connect emotionally with your listeners.
- Organize and focus your message.
- Communicate the gospel more effectively.

Communicating with Bold Assurance Kit includes everything necessary for a comprehensive group or individual study of *Communicating with Bold Assurance:* one workbook, one leader guide, four videotapes, and four audiocassette tapes. (Workbook and leader guide are available separately.) This eight-session study includes personal daily assignments and weekly group sessions during which you will view Bert's video seminar, followed by small-group discussions with exercises, support, and prayer.

Resources:
- *Kit* (ISBN 0-6330-0332-8)
- *Workbook* (ISBN 0-6330-0333-6)
- *Leader Guide* (ISBN 0-6330-0334-4)

To order the above resources call 1 (800) 458-2772.